Most politicians of both major parties totally ignore the Constitution. Generation after generation of politicians has expanded federal powers at the expense of state government authority and individual liberty. Judges have allowed this usurpation of power to continue unchecked.

James Anthony argues that a new political party is needed, a party that consists of individuals who recognize that the Constitution gives the federal government limited powers.

Millions of Americans have awakened to what is going on in their country. Perhaps it is not too late to turn the ship of state around.

— Robert W. McGee, professor, PhDs in economics, ethics, political philosophy, politics, law (JD & PhD), and more

THE
CONSTITUTION
NEEDS A
GOOD PARTY

THE
CONSTITUTION
NEEDS A
GOOD PARTY

GOOD GOVERNMENT
COMES FROM
GOOD BOUNDARIES

JAMES ANTHONY

np
Neuwoehner Press
St. Peters

The Constitution Needs a Good Party: Good Government Comes from Good Boundaries

For information about this title or to order other books and/or electronic media, contact the publisher:
Neuwoehner Press
28 Ellington Oaks Ct.
St. Peters, MO 63376

Library of Congress Control Number: 2017917000

ISBNs: 978-1-948177-00-9 (Hardcover)
          978-1-948177-01-6 (Trade paperback)
          978-1-948177-02-3 (EPUB E-book)
          978-1-948177-03-0 (Mobi E-book)

Printed in the United States of America

Publisher's Cataloging-In-Publication Data

Names: Anthony, James, 1959–
Title: The Constitution needs a good party : good government
    comes from good boundaries / James Anthony.
Description: St. Peters, MO : Neuwoehner Press, [2018] |
    Includes bibliographical references and index.
Identifiers: ISBN 9781948177009 (hardcover) | ISBN
    9781948177016 (trade paperback) | ISBN 9781948177023
    (ePub) | ISBN 9781948177030 (eReader)
Subjects: LCSH: Political parties--United States. | United States--
    Politics and government. | United States. Constitution. |
    United States. Declaration of Independence.
Classification: LCC JK2265 .A58 2018 (print) | LCC JK2265
    (ebook) | DDC 324.273--dc23

Contents

FIGURES

TABLES

PREFACE

THE AMERICAN COLONISTS had a problem. Their forefathers had come to a new land to practice their chosen religion in freedom, to make a living, to build better lives for themselves and their children. In this remote place, a long journey by sailing ship away from the rule of their previous nations, they at first struggled to survive. They organized minimal village and colony governments, and they paid little tax. Taxes as a percentage of gross domestic product for Great Britain's people were almost 20%, but taxes for the colonists were just 1% to 2%.[1]

This freed the colonists to build up per-capita income purchasing power to where it exceeded that of Great Britain's people by a spectacular 68%.[2]

This prosperity made Great Britain's rulers want more from the colonists. The colonists were understandably nervous that they could lose this good thing they had going.[3] They were very sensitive to the rulers' encroachments, and they were determined to keep things freer and better. They succeeded. After the American Revolutionary War, the colonists' secret to staying independent and prospering further turned out to be the Constitution.

The Constitution was drafted and ratified by people who had hands-on working knowledge of various colony and state governments, and of the national government under the Articles of Confederation.

In the Constitution, the states delegated to the national government a small number of powers: chiefly powers relevant to war and powers to ensure that people in various states can do business together freely. All powers not delegated to the national government were either retained by the state governments or retained by the people. This federalism helps different regions' governments differ helpfully, so that different regions' people get more of the locally-adapted government that they mostly want, and they get less of the one-size-fits-all government that they more often don't want. Under federalism, the choices that are more contentious get controlled more locally: religious choices that affect the eternal fate of one's soul are controlled by individuals; punishments for murder are controlled by state governments; freedom to sell beef across state lines is controlled by the national government. Fewer controls are imposed across-the-board on everyone everywhere, so fewer policies need to be fought about.[4]

The Constitution works by separating national lawmaking, national law enforcing, national case judging, and state roles, by defining role boundaries. These boundaries are to be secured by the people in these roles, by countering each other using various offsetting powers. If these offsetting powers are fully used, then individuals' rights are fully secured from abuses by government people. The government people limit the government.[5]

The United States of America long had a reasonably limited government compared to their gross national product: through 1913, total government revenues at all government levels as a percentage of GNP were 4% to 8%.[6]

The USA's constitutionally self-limited government kept Americans free to grow to lead the world. The nation's growth brought the world good things that were new in history: more people, more resources, better sanitation, better nutrition, better health, greater longevity, better quality of life, better environmental quality.[7]

Even as these gains were being realized, various bypasses around the Constitution started to gain the momentum to blow past the built-in self-controls on the national government. Sure enough, by 1922 the government percentage of GNP had jumped to 13%. By 1946, the government percentage of GNP had jumped to 30%.[6]

Such percentages combine many disparate government activities. Some government activities protect property rights; other government activities destroy property rights.[8] Activities that reduce or destroy property rights are predominantly what's added as governments get big. In the case of the jumps in government funding that were noted above, these included funds to return to government exercise of absolute power that worked much like the power that was once exercised by kings, and that therefore was specifically designed to be prevented by the Constitution. These end-arounds to bypass the Constitution were collectively rebranded as modern government and are now called the administrative state (or in short, agencies). This state that was reintroduced by the self-named Progressives soon boasted an infrastructure of academics, fawning support from media, and major proponents in both main parties, which together gave this state huge staying power. For many, many years the administrative state was not called plainly what it was: a throwback; the return of the absolute power that had been wielded by kings.[9] Used to its fullest extent, such government power had in the past unjustly taken away men's freedom and men's lives. Once reintroduced in America, its impact grew strong. The 1946 figure above included a national government percentage of GNP that had jumped to 22%.[6]

This was higher than the level in Great Britain that had sparked the American Revolution.

The jumps in government spending by 1922 and by 1946 had followed the two world wars. This illustrates the ratchet effect on government growth: never letting a crisis go to waste.[10]

Drops in government spending are harder to study. They happen less frequently, and under circumstances that vary.

Government spending was lower in the American colonies compared to in Great Britain because the American colonies were initially hard places in which to stay alive. Government spending in America was kept lower for many years by a succession of factors: by great delays in transatlantic communications using sailing ships, by the American Revolutionary War, by the Constitution.

Government spending in the former countries of the Soviet Union became lower after the Soviet Union collapsed, as people in these governments transitioned out of owning and centrally controlling production and distribution of goods and services, and transitioned into more-limited roles.

The advent of smaller governments in the American colonies, the maintenance of smaller governments in pre-1900 America, and the transitions to smaller governments in the former countries of the Soviet Union have been the subjects of isolated studies. But such isolated studies have not made clear a path for peacefully making the national government in the United States of America step down significantly in size and in destructive impact.

The Constitution Needs a Good Party diagnoses the root-cause problem: the national government has been staying ratcheted up in size because in election after election, a reliable strong majority of the people elected from the two main political parties consists of people who don't use their powers under the Constitution to keep other government people in check. Look past their deceptive sound and fury, look at their votes and their policy outcomes, and it's clear that they're colluding. They're partners in crime.

This book offers the single best cure: to develop at least one party that has internal self-controls like the national government self-controls provided by the Constitution.

Given at least one party that functions well, the party's grassroots people will be able to nominate candidates who will follow the Constitution. Such constitutional-conservative candidates—starting with George Washington and Ronald Reagan—have made it onto general-election ballots in the past, and they ended up winning by first-term electoral college percentage margins that were the highest ever.[11] Once at least one party starts reliably nominating such candidates in substantial numbers, the American people will elect these candidates in substantial numbers.

The more fully that at least one major party's representatives use their powers under the Constitution, the more fully the national government will be self-limited.

Then people in different regions will be able to stay different and at the same time stay happier with one another. They—we—will stay secure together, and will work together better than ever.

PART 1

A GOOD PARTY

THE SUCCESSFUL LAUNCH of the Republican Party followed from two features: a widely-shared bedrock philosophy (republican participatory government), and unique major policies (anti-slavery, anti-Southern elite power, and anti-Catholic).[12]

Both a widely-shared bedrock philosophy and unique major policies can readily be built into a new major party. The party just needs the right structure.

This is shown below as follows. We see that the current parties' structures consistently deliver majorities of representatives who don't follow the Constitution. We see that the Constitution provides a much better-designed model for a party's structure.

Next, various well-designed components of our government's structure are used as models for a new party name, party declaration, party constitution, and party laws.

Given this picture, we can envision how this party's processes will teach this party's people how to follow the Constitution's processes. We can envision how the current parties' people and the new party's people will most likely interact during the transition period when the new party is growing. And we can envision how such a new party and the Constitution will work together hand-in-hand once the dust settles.

The first step toward the solution is to understand that the problem is our current parties.

CHAPTER 1

TAILS WAG DOG

THE CONSTITUTION PROVIDES a structure defined by roles and the associated powers. Individual liberty and sovereignty are protected from government people only secondarily through the Bill of Rights (the Constitution's first ten amendments). Individual rights are protected from government people primarily by relying on government people to secure the role boundaries.[5] But most government people from the parties that have existed to date have not secured the role boundaries.

Their role boundary violations have been of two kinds: failing to assert their own role boundaries, and disrespecting other people's role boundaries. They have left undone the things that they ought to have done, and they have done those things that they ought not to have done.[13] They don't do their jobs.

Parties are the source of government representatives, and government representatives control policy actions. Small party-government actions produce big government actions. The tails wag the dog. Parties have high leverage over the government. And high leverage that's exerted badly works out badly.

The current control of the Senate by Progressives, for example, is shown in Figure 1 below. The senators' Progressive Scores there are 100% minus the senators' Conservative Review Liberty Scores.[14] The Democrats and Independents are pure Progressive. Half of the Republicans are mixed Progressive, and half are mixed constitutional conservative. Since 1/2 of the Senate is pure-Progressive Democrats and Independents, and 1/2 (=2/4) of the Senate is mixed-Progressive Republicans, in total the Senate is 3/4 Progressive.

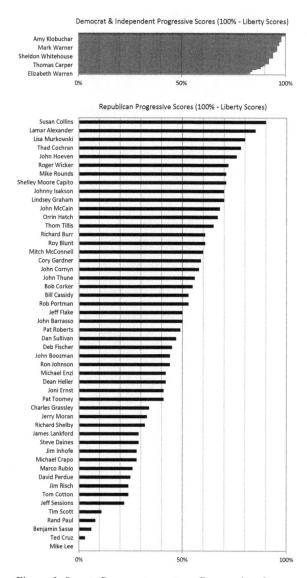

Figure 1. Senate Democrats are pure Progressive. Senate Republican leaders and median members are mixed Progressive.[14]

The substantial Progressive presence in the House, together with the Progressive lock on the Senate, means that regardless of whether Congress is controlled by Democrats or Republicans, Congress is controlled by Progressives. One-party Progressive rule is locked in. In fact, one-party Progressive rule has been locked in throughout what is now acknowledged to have been *The Progressives' Century*.[15]

Using law professor Randy Barnett's defining nomenclature from *Our Republican Constitution*, Progressives follow the "democratic Constitution."[16] They claim that in the Constitution, "We the People" means the democratic majority, and the democratic majority's will determines the meaning of the Constitution.

That's their cover story. Actually, the so-called democratic majority that they use as a pretext has no voice, because the so-called democratic majority has no viable alternative to being represented by Progressive majorities in government. Government policy is controlled by a small group of elected representatives and unelected judges, a tight-knit group that's kept in place by the Progressive-controlled Democratic and Republican parties' candidate-selection processes.

The parties select candidates using Progressive news coverage, Progressive campaign finance rules, Progressive debate questions, few caucuses as offsetting influences, primary calendars elevating Progressive states and territories, open primaries favoring Progressives, winner-take-all voting favoring the initially better-known Progressives, and simultaneous primaries favoring the initially better-known Progressives. This selection process is kept as-is because this process satisfies the interests of the parties' leaders, and because the leaders have the control of this process concentrated in their hands.

The resulting general-election matchups for Congress pit pure-Progressive Democrats against many mixed-Progressive Republicans and some mixed-constitutional-conservative Republicans. The resulting general-election matchups for president nearly always pit a pure-Progressive Democrat against a mixed-Progressive Republican. The resulting Progressive majorities are said to represent us.

But once they're in government, the Progressive philosophy, at its core, is to simply ignore the controls that the Constitution places on government people, and to do as they see fit.[17]

No spending seems too extreme; no action seems too extreme; no moral or social deviation seems too extreme.

National-government gross public debt as a percentage of GDP for 1792 to 2015 is graphed in Figure 2 below.

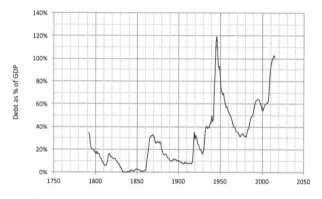

Figure 2. USA national-government gross public debt as a percentage of GDP for 1792–2015[18]

A close look at the figure offers great insight across history.

Every major war, producing debt peaks in 1869, 1919, and 1946,[18] came under Progressive antecedents[19] or Progressives.

Every peacetime debt jump, beginning in 1929, 1981, and 2001, came under Progressives or under Progressive Congresses. Not one of these peacetime debt jumps has yet been fully reversed.

The latest peacetime debt jump raised the debt as a percentage of GDP from 55% to 101%.[18]

When total debt exceeded 60% of GDP in various countries studied, any new stimulus spending signaled that spending reductions might be needed later and might be sudden and large, so investors took their money and ran. It turned out that for these countries with high debt, stimulus spending of one dollar was estimated to cause a short-term output change of close to 0 dollars (that is, it was an immediate total loss), and was estimated to cause a long-term output change of −3 dollars![20]

Progressives have pushed us into fragility well beyond what we've gone through in any prior peacetime, even prior peacetimes that precipitated major wars.

In data that spanned 8 centuries, really-bad government management occurred repeatedly, and it repeatedly ended badly.[21] Dyin' ain't much of a living.[22]

Big government debts come from big governments. Big governments during peacetimes produce recessions that are deep and long: more pain that people feel.[23]

During the last peacetime debt jump, when people were polled on how they feel about "our system of government and how well it works" from

2001 to 2016, the total who were dissatisfied rose from 30% to 64%, and the portion who were very dissatisfied rose from 9% to 33%, as shown in Figure 3 below.[24]

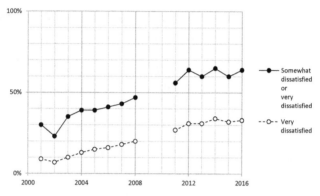

Figure 3. Dissatisfaction with "our system of government and how well it works"[24]

These dissatisfied people likely include many potential new-party voters, given that in the latest polling, self-identified conservatives and self-identified moderates each significantly out-numbered self-identified liberals, respectively 36% to 25% and 34% to 25%.[25]

The most-recent constitutional-conservative president, Ronald Reagan, won by electoral college percentage margins that both times topped those of every president since.

Reagan's margin in 1984 was only exceeded in 1936, 1820, 1792, and 1789.[11] This massive constitutional-conservative victory in recent times, just 34 years ago, has been exceeded by a Progressive victory only one time ever, a distant 82 years ago.

Reagan's first-term margin in 1980 has only been exceeded by that of one other president, George Washington, in 1789. Washington's and Reagan's massive constitutional-conservative first-term victories have not been matched by those of any Progressives.

In recent years many people have repeatedly voted for the general-election candidates of the major party that promised the greatest-available possible change in the direction of the government. The somewhat-less-Progressive Republicans gained control of the House in 2010, the Senate in 2014, the presidency in 2016, and both state houses and the governorship in 25 states by 2016.[26]

And yet Obamacare-type central controls remain. Plans keep rolling along on a new $1.5 trillion stimulus. The current major parties have not delivered a substantive change in the direction of the government, and will not. These parties' parasitic track record in the past will stretch out into the future for as long as the host nation limps along.

The current major parties' Progressive lean is guaranteed by these parties' poor internal control structures.

Chapter 2

Nation's Structure Is Best Model for Party's Structure

The internal control structures of our political parties have so far been surpassed by the internal control structure of the nation.

To be sure, the entities to be controlled are different in scale and scope. The nation's government is tasked, above all, with providing military protection;[27] a party's government is tasked above all with providing candidate-selection processes.

But just as the nation's government, in order to serve its citizens, needs to have the power to do grave harm, a party's government, in order to serve its party citizens, also needs to have the power to do grave harm. The tails need to have the power to wag the dog.

Unavoidably, then, the people's rights need to be protected not only by the nation's government structure, but also by at least one party's government structure. The best-available government structure is defined by the nation's name the United States of America, by the Declaration of Independence, and by the Constitution.

Prior party names have been rendered deceptive by inadequate party structures. That will be changed by providing a resilient party structure and robust party laws that will protect and defend the party's brand name.

Much of the party's structure can follow straightforwardly from a line-by-line reading of the Declaration and the Constitution, so here we will focus on key points and nonobvious analogies. Given that the nation's government performs many functions, much has been done to defy the Constitution, and therefore much time is taken here to describe this defiance in the party declaration's grievances. Given that a party's government can perform just the single function of candidate selection, less needs to be done to build a party well from the start(!), so less time is needed here to cover the party constitution and the party laws.

As the first step in building the party to function well, both now and in the future, some care is taken here to advocate a party name that's uncorrupted and that's precisely descriptive.

CHAPTER 3

NATION'S NAME IS BEST
MODEL FOR PARTY'S NAME

THE UNITED STATES OF AMERICA is a name
that's specific and deliberate. America is the geo-
graphic place, the states are explicitly-named
entities, and the nation is described as these states
united. The name reinforces that the states are
semi-autonomous, and that they're united for
limited purposes (above all, military protection).[27]

The republican Constitution party is a name
that's also specific and deliberate: this is the party
that follows the "republican Constitution," which
is defined securely in Professor Randy Barnett's
Our Republican Constitution.[28] If democratic majorities were sovereign, and if individual rights were
determined by democratic majorities, then the

17

Constitution would be a democratic Constitution. But if individuals are sovereign, and if individual rights are secured by a republican form of government, then the Constitution is a republican Constitution. This latter understanding is the correct understanding, as shown by Professor Barnett.

The nation was formed with the Declaration of Independence. In our governing documents, the very first words after the Declaration of Independence are the opening words in the Constitution, "We the People." "We the People" can only mean the people defined by the Declaration.

The Declaration in no way suggests that we are a people collectively ruled by the will of a democratic majority. The Declaration explains that we are sovereign individuals endowed by our Creator with certain inalienable rights, and that our national government is instituted to secure these rights. A national government that follows the will of a democratic majority does not and cannot secure each sovereign individual's preexisting rights.[29] A national government that follows the will of a majority-Progressive slate of candidates is even farther away from securing each sovereign individual's pre-existing rights. A democratic majority is a large group to satisfy, so their government has some limits; Progressive representatives are a small group to satisfy, so their government has few limits.

A republican government will secure sovereign individuals' rights only to the extent that the government people vigorously assert their own role boundaries, and vigorously respect other people's role boundaries.

A republican Constitution party will secure sovereign individuals' rights only to the extent that its candidate-selection processes select candidates who will vigorously assert their own role boundaries, and who will vigorously respect other people's role boundaries.

A party's candidate-selection processes come from the party's government. Just as a national government can secure individual rights only by having a suitable structure of roles and associated powers, a party government can secure individual rights only by having a suitable structure of roles and associated powers. It's only natural, then, that a suitable party government structure can best be designed by repurposing the best-available model of a structure of roles and associated powers.

Despite the vulnerability of the national government if every party's structure is bad, the best-available model of a structure of roles and associated powers is still the model provided by the national government's Declaration of Independence and the national government's Constitution.

Chapter 4

Nation's Declaration Is Best Model for Party's Declaration

THE PARTY INDEPENDENCE being declared will be independence not from the Republican Party, but from all prior or existing parties.

The party declaration's preamble will include a concise summary of how the Constitution protects rights:

Individual sovereign rights are protected through the Constitution separating the legislative, executive, and judicial functions; through the Constitution providing offsetting powers to people responsible for performing these functions; and through the people in government vigorously asserting their powers against

21

other people in government, and vigorously respecting others' powers. Failing to assert one's own powers, or failing to respect others' powers, defies the Constitution, which usurps individual sovereign rights.

The party declaration's grievances will provide clear examples of unconstitutional national governance that has resulted from poor party structures that select poor candidates. The grievances will also provide further clear examples of poor party governance.

Congressmen in prior parties have passed, and have left in place, so-called laws that effectively cannot be read, in defiance of the Constitution.

A congressman who can't fully understand a bill in the time he considers it and who signs it anyway, or who leaves in place such a law, is not representing his constituency, not wittingly. Review of prior law is a high obligation of congressmen; they owe this to their constituents, since, after all, review of prior law is a high burden on constituents. To cut this burden down, laws need to be read and then either repealed, or written better as described next.

Congressmen in prior parties have passed, and have left in place, so-called laws that direct the executive branch or the judicial branch, in defiance of the Constitution.

Statements embedded in laws that set timetables, otherwise direct executive actions, or direct judicial actions (other than per Article III) are not statements of law, but rather are unconstitutional crossings of role boundaries. Laws are purely rules and penalties on conduct that's impermissible.[30] And nothing more.

Congressmen in prior parties have passed, and have left in place, so-called laws that delegate legislative authority to issue so-called regulations that plainly have the force of laws, in defiance of the Constitution.

Writing laws trumps executing laws, and executing laws trumps judging cases. The Constitution reserves the legislative power to Congress alone, so any so-called laws that delegate legislative power to others are unlawful. The administrative state is unlawful.[31] When congressmen can repeal such so-called laws and they don't, they become complicit parties to the so-called laws and to the so-called regulations.

Congressmen in prior parties have passed, and have left in place, so-called laws that are misleading, providing support for others to legislate by interpretation, in defiance of the Constitution.

Laws, again, are purely rules and penalties on conduct that's impermissible.[30] Rules are actionable, since facts can be determined, and penalties are actionable, since consequences can be imposed, so laws are made up entirely of content that's actionable.

If, on the other hand, something is included that isn't a rule and isn't a penalty, that content isn't law. Such non-law content makes it harder to recognize when a law's rules and penalties aren't clear and complete. Such non-law content can invite other people to fill in the vacuum. Often, such non-law content even misdirects people to fill in the vacuum. In such ways, such non-law content is misleading.

For example, new drug approval statutorily requires "substantial evidence that the drug will have the effect it purports or is represented to have."[32] In this law, "substantial evidence" is misleading, because FDA people can constantly raise the bar, which lets them reduce the number of new drugs, reducing the FDA people's risk of approving a drug that later turns out to have harmful side effects.[33] Meanwhile, "will have the effect it … is represented to have" is misleading, because drug manufacturers can promise virtually no efficacy and deliver virtually no efficacy.

People pay heavy prices for this misleading law. Drugs that would have been invented don't get invented. Drugs that would have saved lives or greatly relieved suffering don't get approved for years.[34]

Laws have consequences, and the consequences can be deadly serious when laws have misleading content. Misleading content includes titles, goals, context, legislative history, and any other content that's not actionable.

Congressmen in prior parties have passed, and have left in place, so-called laws that exceed the enumerated powers, in defiance of the Constitution.

The Constitution explicitly enumerates the national government's powers so that states can represent their residents' preferences better,[35] and so that the explicit limits on the national government leave individual rights more secure. The Constitution is a legal contract. As long as the contract isn't amended to explicitly change this core structure, grabbing any other powers for the national government is illegal.

Congressmen in prior parties have passed, and have left in place, so-called laws that permit and fund abortions, in defiance of the Declaration and the Constitution.

The Declaration affirms and the Constitution protects[36] individuals' inalienable right to life, which abortions take away.

The Constitution gives no explicit power to permit or fund abortions. The government permits and funds abortions only through unconstitutional ongoing actions and inactions of congresses, presidents and governors, and judges.

The government people in each role have constitutional powers to independently stop abortions. Congressmen are bound by oath or affirmation to support the Constitution,[37] and congressmen violate this oath when they leave in place or enact legislation that treats unconstitutional judicial opinions as constitutional. In analogous ways, state legislators, presidents and governors, and national and state judges each violate the Constitution when they each do not act individually to stop abortions.

Congressmen in prior parties have passed, and have left in place, so-called laws authorizing fractional-reserve banking, paper money not backed 100% by gold or silver, and a central bank, in defiance of the Declaration and the Constitution.

The Declaration affirms individuals' inalienable right to liberty, which includes a right to one's own property that is acquired through one's own labor. The Constitution enumerates only the power to coin money. Government and government-crony[38] money manipulations stop people in business from offering higher-quality money, which would greatly limit economic cycles and pain.[39, 40, 41, 42, 43] Government people tax us without representation, behind-the-scenes, by taking away from us the natural appreciation in value of our money as our productivity improves,[44] and by further devaluing our money through inflation.[45] They force on us a needless, increasing risk of hyperinflation.[21]

Congressmen in prior parties have failed to declare war and have passed, and have left in place, so-called laws authorizing violent actions that plainly are war, in defiance of the Constitution.

The Constitution requires government people to maintain boundaries that structure the decision to engage in war: congressmen declare war; the president conducts war. All elected representatives are engaged.

These boundaries were established by people who had won a war.

When elected representatives maintain these boundaries, we fight less often, we're better prepared economically,[46] all our elected representatives are accountable for victory, we can (and morally we should) completely destroy the offending enemy governments and their enablers, and our potential enemies attack less.

Congressmen in prior parties have passed, and have left in place, so-called laws creating block grants that use monetary incentives to control state actions, in defiance of the Constitution.

The Constitution reserves all unenumerated powers for the states. So-called laws that use block grants always in practice grab unenumerated powers, and always use monetary incentives to exert control over states' actions, doubly violating states' rights. In the 1996 welfare reform, for example, the national government continued its grab of unenumerated power to provide income support,[47] and the national government used conditional monetary grants to control states through explicit mandates, financial penalties, financial incentives for states to appropriate new funding, and other mechanisms.[48]

Senators in prior parties have failed to pass bills by simple majorities, in defiance of the Constitution.

The Senate has as its president the Vice President, who has "… no Vote, unless they be equally divided." The Senate vote can be equally divided only under simple-majority voting.

Also, the normal legislative process is that "Every Bill which shall have passed the House of Representatives and the Senate … shall … be presented to the President." The word "passed" with no further conditions meant passed by the simple majorities present. This was the established practice as confirmed in detail in the reference cited here, and confirmed in further detail in three references cited there: the two English legal dictionaries that existed in 1787, and Noah Webster's dictionary of 1828.[49]

When change is for the better, like after the Soviet Union dissolved, fast and extensive change produces greatly-superior results. Fast change overcomes the ability of people who are already in power to dig in. Fast change therefore helps make sure that change is able to occur, so things do get better.

Former Soviet-bloc countries used different approaches to achieving economic freedom after the fall of the USSR. Their progress over 25 years is plotted in Figure 4 below.

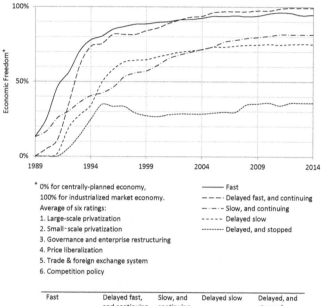

⁺ 0% for centrally-planned economy,
100% for industrialized market economy.
Average of six ratings:
1. Large-scale privatization
2. Small-scale privatization
3. Governance and enterprise restructuring
4. Price liberalization
5. Trade & foreign exchange system
6. Competition policy

——— Fast
— — — Delayed fast, and continuing
— · — · — Slow, and continuing
- - - - - Delayed slow
········ Delayed, and stopped

Fast	Delayed fast, and continuing	Slow, and continuing	Delayed slow	Delayed, and stopped
Central European	*Baltic*	*Southeast European*	*Former Soviet more-reformed*	*Former Soviet less-reformed*
Poland	Estonia	Bosnia	Russia	Belarus
Czech Republic	Latvia	Serbia	Ukraine	Uzbekistan
(data to 2007)	Lithuania	Romania	Moldova	Turkmenistan
Slovak Republic		Albania	Georgia	
Hungary		Macedonia	Armenia	
Slovenia		Bulgaria	Azerbaijan	
Croatia			Kazakhstan	
			Kyrgyzstan	
			Tajikistan	
			Mongolia	

Figure 4. After the Berlin Wall was torn down, fast change brought good results fast, and the progress kept up.[50, 51]

The upper two lines show the groups of countries that moved the most quickly. For these fast-changing countries, the gains in economic freedom were rapid and large for 5 years. From there, the gains continued steadily, so that these countries maintained a sizable lead over the other countries for period for which data were available—another 20 years.[50]

When change is for the worse, like with Obamacare, fast and extensive change also produces greatly-superior final results. Fast and extensive change for the worse provides superior visibility and accountability, and these bring about faster and more-extensive reversal.

In the case of Obamacare, the delayed implementation was a feature designed to reduce visibility and accountability by delaying the full effects until after the new regime was entrenched; in implementing Obamacare, fast change would have made the results more acutely toxic. Simply rolling back to the pre-Obamacare regime would make it legal for insurers to quickly return to pre-Obamacare plans that offered lower premiums, lower deductibles, more providers, and more competition.

Senators in prior parties have refused to advise and consent on treaties negotiated by presidents, and congressmen in prior parties have passed or have left in place so-called laws supporting the treaties, in defiance of the Constitution.

Progressive President Barack Obama made a treaty with Iran. Progressive senators did not bring the treaty up for a vote. Progressive congressmen passed a so-called law that bypassed the requirement for advice and consent by 2/3 of the senators present, and allowed Progressive presidents to execute the unapproved treaty.

Presidents and senators in prior parties have appointed and confirmed judges who have claimed power to decide the constitutionality of laws, and congressmen in prior parties have not impeached and convicted the judges, in defiance of the Constitution.

Congress has all legislative authority. The Supreme Court mostly has appellate jurisdiction on individual cases, with exceptions and under regulations made by Congress. The inferior courts are ordained and established by Congress. Judges claiming power to invalidate laws are attempting to legislate. When these judges are not impeached and convicted, this inaction defies the Constitution.

Presidents and senators in prior parties have appointed and confirmed judges who have asserted positive rights to compel people to give up private property, and congressmen in prior parties have not impeached and convicted the judges, in defiance of the Declaration and the Constitution.

Primarily the government structure of offsetting powers provided by the Constitution, and secondarily the Bill of Rights, guards inalienable individual rights,[13] among which is liberty. Individual liberty is denied to whatever extent private property—which is acquired through one's own labor—is taken away by force from individuals, for example through taxes, in order that property can be transferred to people in government or to other individuals.

Presidents and senators in prior parties have appointed and confirmed administrators who have committed unconstitutional actions, and congressmen in prior parties have not impeached and convicted the administrators, in defiance of the Constitution.

The IRS's Lois Lerner and John Koskinen broadly denied free-speech rights, affecting elections, and congressmen didn't impeach them and convict them.

Presidents in prior parties have signed and executed, and have continued to execute, so-called laws that effectively cannot be read, in defiance of the Constitution.

Like congressmen, presidents are bound by oath or affirmation to support the Constitution.[37] Complying with unconstitutional laws violates this duty.[52] Presidents acting constitutionally will not sign bills into laws that are unconstitutional, and will not execute new or existing laws that are unconstitutional. Constitutional execution of executive power is not a rubber stamp. "The buck stops here."[53]

Presidents in prior parties have signed and executed, and have continued to execute, so-called laws that direct the executive branch or the judicial branch, in defiance of the Constitution.

Presidents in prior parties have signed and executed, and have continued to execute, so-called laws that delegate legislative authority to issue so-called regulations that plainly have the force of laws, in defiance of the Constitution.

Presidents in prior parties have signed and executed, and have continued to execute, so-called laws that are misleading, providing support for others to legislate by interpretation, in defiance of the Constitution.

Presidents in prior parties have signed and executed, and have continued to execute, so-called laws that exceed the enumerated powers, in defiance of the Constitution.

Presidents in prior parties have signed and executed, and have continued to execute, so-called laws that permit and fund abortions, in defiance of the Declaration and the Constitution.

Presidents in prior parties have signed and executed, and have continued to execute, so-called laws authorizing fractional-reserve banking, paper money not backed 100% by gold or silver, and a central bank, in defiance of the Declaration and the Constitution.

Presidents in prior parties, without declarations of war, have executed, and have continued to execute, nonemergency violent actions that are plainly war, in defiance of the Constitution.

Presidents in prior parties have signed and executed, and have continued to execute, so-called laws creating block grants that use monetary incentives to control state actions, in defiance of the Constitution.

State congressmen in prior parties have complied with so-called laws that violate the Constitution, in defiance of the Constitution.

Like the national congressmen and presidents, the state congressmen, executive officers, and judicial officers are bound by oath or affirmation to support the Constitution,[37] and complying with unconstitutional laws violates this duty.[52] It was the state people who originally delegated specific powers to the national government, and it is the state people or the people themselves to whom all other powers are reserved.[54]

When the national government people attempt to grab powers, the powers they grab belong to the states, or to the states' people. State people's failures to use their constitutional powers deny their people the foundational layer of protection for their people's sovereign rights.

State congressmen in prior parties have passed, and have left in place, so-called laws that permit and fund abortions, in defiance of the Declaration and the Constitution.

Governors and state attorneys general in prior parties have complied with so-called laws that violate the Constitution, in defiance of the Constitution.

Governors and state attorneys general in prior parties have signed and executed, and have continued to execute, so-called laws that permit and fund abortions, in defiance of the Declaration and the Constitution.

State judges in prior parties have complied with so-called laws that violate the Constitution, in defiance of the Constitution.

State judges have complied with so-called laws that permit and fund abortions, in defiance of the Declaration and the Constitution.

People in prior parties have permitted open primaries, favoring the selection of Progressive candidates, who defy the Constitution.

State-by-state comparisons show that in the Republican Party, which is mixed Progressive and therefore is more in play, open primaries normally deliver greater percentages of the vote to more-Progressive candidates.

People in prior parties have permitted primaries, favoring the selection of Progressive candidates, who defy the Constitution.

State-by-state comparisons show that in the mixed-Progressive Republican Party, primaries normally deliver greater percentages of the vote to more-Progressive candidates than caucuses deliver. Primaries take less time commitment and involve less interaction with more-informed voters, so candidates can get farther on name recognition alone. Name recognition is greater for incumbents due to ongoing news exposure, and due to campaign finance laws that give incumbents preferential treatment that enables their media buys to be larger.

People in prior parties have permitted winner-take-all and winner-take-most primaries or caucuses, favoring the selection of previously-elected, better-known Progressive candidates, who defy the Constitution.

Greater-than-proportional weighting of votes allows Progressive candidates, who are better recognized early on, to build leads early on that are harder for less-recognized constitutional-conservative candidates to overcome when their name recognition builds up later.

People in prior parties have permitted multiple primaries or caucuses on the same day, favoring the selection of previously-elected, better-known Progressive candidates, who defy the Constitution.

Like winner-take-all contests, same-day contests favor Progressive candidates who are better recognized at the time of these contests, early on.

People in prior parties have directed campaign funds to favor Progressive candidates, who defy the Constitution.

Campaign funds have been collected from a broad spectrum of constitutional conservatives and other party members, and then used to help a narrow slice of Progressive candidates (who often are vulnerable to challenges because they are less popular with voters).

People in prior parties have broken party laws by rejecting petitions to vote on party law changes, in order to favor the selection of Progressive candidates, who defy the Constitution.

Party rules were broken at the 2016 Republican Convention to prevent a roll-call vote for or against newly-proposed rules that further centralized power.[55]

At the time of the Declaration, the king's usurpations were clear, but the government's functioning was unclear.

Now the government people's dysfunctions are clear, and the prior party people's defiance is clear.

CHAPTER 5

NATION'S CONSTITUTION IS BEST MODEL FOR PARTY'S CONSTITUTION

THE CONSTITUTION DOESN'T right usurpations by prescribing policy, but rather by providing a structure that protects individual rights by pitting government people against one another.

In the same way, the republican Constitution party constitution won't right the dysfunction and defiance by prescribing policy, but rather by providing a structure that protects the Constitution by pitting party-government people against one another.

Note that a national government has several complex major functions, including providing military protection.[27] A national-party government has just one simple major function: defining the process for national-candidate selection.

Using the Constitution as the model, and tailoring for candidate selection, will provide the following republican Constitution party constitution.

All legislative powers herein granted shall be vested in a congress of the republican Constitution party, which shall consist of a house of representatives and a senate.

The house of representatives shall be composed of members chosen every second year by the party people by congressional district.

The Republican Party lacks a people's house. This body will run for election frequently, so this will be the body that's most responsive to the party's members.

The senate shall be composed of two senators from each state, chosen by the state party congress for six years, and each senator shall have one vote.

All bills for raising revenue shall originate in the house of representatives, but the senate may propose or concur with amendments as on other bills.

The congress shall have power to solicit and collect donations;

to arrange national party meetings;

to set schedules for, and national party controls on, state party selection of candidates for the national government;

This intrusion on state party sovereignty doesn't follow from the Constitution, but is needed in the party constitution to keep more-Progressive states from running open contests, primaries, or non-proportional voting that would select less-pure national candidates, damaging brand purity.

— and

to make all party laws which shall be necessary and proper for carrying into execution the foregoing powers, and all other powers vested by this constitution in the republican Constitution party government, or in any department or officer thereof.

The executive power shall be vested in a president of the republican Constitution party. He shall hold his office during the term of four years, and, together with the vice president, chosen for the same term, be elected, as follows … [per the Constitution].

He shall have power, by and with the advice and consent of the senate, to make party-sanctioned debate schedules, provided two thirds of the senators concur.

The judicial power of the republican Constitution party shall be vested in one supreme court.

The judicial power shall extend to all cases, in law and equity, arising under this constitution, the laws of the republican Constitution party, and party-sanctioned debate schedules made, or which shall be made, under their authority.

The republican Constitution party shall have no platform.

This amendment will stake out a clear boundary between the party and the candidates. The party government will be fully accountable for national-government candidate-selection processes; the candidates will be fully accountable for their roles in government processes.

As shown, the party's constitution will establish separate national-party roles, will enumerate very-limited national powers, and will forbid establishing a platform.

The party's constitution will also replicate other parts of the nation's Constitution that have analogies for a party: further applicable parts of Articles I, II, and III regarding legislative, executive, and judicial powers; applicable parts of Articles IV, V, VI, and VII regarding states, amendment, supreme law, and ratification; and applicable parts of Amendments 10, 12, 17, 22, 23, and 26 regarding state powers, presidential election, election of senators, presidential term limits, DC electors, and voting age.

The national government has complex major functions, so it was not feasible to accompany the Constitution with a functional body of advisable national-government law.

In contrast, a national-party government just defines the process for national-candidate selection, so it is feasible to accompany the national-party constitution with a functional body of advisable national-party law. This body of national-party law is described in the next chapter.

CHAPTER 6

PRIOR PARTIES' LAWLESSNESS IS BEST GUIDE ON PARTY'S LAWS

PRIOR PARTIES' poor candidate-selection practices that aren't changed by the party constitution will be changed by party laws.

The party laws of current parties have shown not what works, but rather what doesn't work. Also, compared to the party constitution, party laws can be enacted and repealed more easily. Since available party models don't work, and since any party laws that are good could be repealed relatively easily, putting requirements into party laws rather than into the party constitution adds risk.

But where the added risk of party laws is acceptable, party laws offer fast reaction, experimentation, and flexibility.

A previously-elected candidate shall qualify to run as a member of the party only if his Conservative Review Liberty Score is a minimum of 80%.

A scoring-measure requirement can improve brand purity.

Available scoring measures rate congressmen based on their voting on current legislation, which is mostly very far from constitutional. Agencies, for instance, write what are effectively laws, which is unconstitutional; but a given vote to fund such agencies will often still be scored by available scoring measures as constitutionally conservative, based on factors other than constitutionality. Because of this, the available scores make candidates' voting look more constitutional than the voting is in reality; the scores do not measure candidates' absolute levels of constitutional conservatism. In the future, we can do better. For now, the available scores do at least sort the candidates.

Given current representatives' performance, a scoring measure that's suitable won't rate most current representatives very high.

By using a scoring measure that's from a single source rather than using an average of scores from multiple sources, any mistakes will be easier to see, and scoring will be easier for representatives to anticipate and to make desirable adjustments for, so that they can improve their scores.

An independent source will be better than an internal party source because an independent source will be more-easily replaceable, and because an independent source will have strong incentives to be forthcoming and user-friendly.

Of the scoring measures that are currently available, the Conservative Review Liberty Score[14] looks the most suitable as a starting point.

A Liberty Score cutoff of 80% will make allowances for some Liberty Score imprecision, which is unavoidable until the new party gains enough control over the agenda to make legislation more constitutional. In the meantime, a cutoff of 80% will require candidates to make 4 Constitution-supporting votes for every 1 Constitution-defying vote, while a cutoff of 70% would only require candidates to make 2.3 Constitution-supporting votes for every 1 Constitution-defying vote.

Party-sanctioned debates shall have no moderators, no commentators from the start to the finish of the debate, and no questions other than the questions asked by the candidates during the debates.

Moderators—and questions from outsiders—alter topics, perspectives, candidates' times, and interactions. Commentators alter voters' impressions.

In the 2016 cycle's candidate-selection debates and forums, the Republican Party people deployed biased media extensively, as shown in Table 1 below. On a Progressive-vs.-constitutional scale, nearly all the media hosts would have rated as moderately to strongly Progressive. Available ratings used a less-informative left-vs.-right scale. Although Republicans are thought of as right-leaning, the Republican Party undermined right-leaning candidates by sanctioning debate control by left-biased media hosts.

Candidates can and should take back this airtime, cover their own priorities, and ask their own questions.

As the party grows, the media and the prior parties won't shut it out forever; the candidates will be news, and content is king.[58]

Table 1. 2016 Republican Party presidential candidate-selection debate & forum schedule bias[56, 57]

Date	Sanctioned	Event	No.	Hosts	Extreme Left	Left	Left-Center	Center	Right-Center	Right	Extreme Right
08/03/15	–	Forum	1	C-SPAN				x			
08/06/15	RNC	Debate	1	Facebook, Fox News		O				X	
09/16/15	RNC	Debate	2	CNN, Salem Radio		X			X		
10/28/15	RNC	Debate	3	CNBC, Westwood One		XO					
11/10/15	RNC	Debate	4	Wall Street Journal, Fox Business					X	O	
11/20/15	–	Forum	2	The Family Leader						o	
12/03/15	–	Forum	3	Republican Jewish Coalition					o		
12/15/15	RNC	Debate	5	CNN, Salem Radio		X			X		
01/09/16	–	Forum	4	Jack Kemp Foundation						o	
01/14/16	RNC	Debate	6	Facebook, Fox Business		O				O	
01/28/16	RNC	Debate	7	Google, Fox News		O				X	
02/06/16	RNC	Debate	8	ABC News, Independent Journal Review		X				X	
02/13/16	RNC	Debate	9	CBS News		X					
02/17/16	–	Forum	5	CNN		x					
02/24/16	–	Forum	6	Fox News						x	
02/25/16	RNC	Debate	10	CNN, Telemundo, Salem Radio		XO			X		
03/03/16	RNC	Debate	11	Fox News						X	
03/09/16	–	Forum	7	Fox News						x	
03/10/16	RNC	Debate	12	CNN, Salem Radio, Washington Times		X			XX		
03/21/16	–	Forum	8	CNN		x					
03/29/16	–	Forum	9	CNN		x					
All dates	RNC	Debates	All hosts			14				10	
All dates	–	Forums	All hosts			4				5	
All dates		Events	All hosts			18				15	

X RNC sanctioned. Bias rating available.
O RNC sanctioned. Bias rating not available.
x Not RNC sanctioned. Bias rating available.
o Not RNC sanctioned. Bias rating not available.

Dashed line shows standard to uphold at various times in candidate-selection process to maintain brand purity. Event hosts to left of dashed line, who harmed brand purity, totaled 18. Event hosts to right of dashed line, who helped brand purity, totaled 15. Only event hosts to right of dashed line, who helped brand purity, would have been agreed to by party-government people and candidates who maintained brand purity.

Candidates for Congress shall be selected using closed caucuses with proportional voting.

Closed voting will limit voting to people who are on record as being more committed to the party's philosophy.

Caucuses will require a greater time commitment, and caucuses will ensure that before a person votes he will get more information from more sources, including from other people who are relatively interested and informed.

Proportional voting will let candidates compete longer, so good candidates who are lesser known can become better known and can win.

The candidate for president shall be selected using closed caucuses with proportional voting, using a candidate electoral college the same in numbers and distribution as the electoral college, and counting only candidate electors from regions represented by the party in the House or Senate.

The candidate electoral college will ensure that every region counted in candidate selection will count in candidate election.

Counting candidate electors only from regions represented by the party will ensure that candidates will be selected only by people who are measurably successful at winning elections and at representing the party in government, who will be likely to more-successfully advance the party and refine its governance in the national government.

State caucuses to select candidates for Congress and president shall be scheduled one state at a time, approximately equally-spaced apart in time, in order of decreasing party strength. The party strength shall be the average of the party proportions of the vote in the most-recent elections for each House and Senate seat in the state, with each election counted as being of equal weight in the average.

As noted previously, caucuses rather than primaries will select the voters who are more active, and will help prepare those voters even better with timely information.

One-state-at-a-time contests will lengthen the selection process, so good candidates who are lesser known can become better known and can win.

Approximately-equal spacing over time will maximize the time available to focus campaigns on each individual state.

The weighting in the average party strength will equal the weighting in the electoral college.

Proceeding in the order of decreasing party strength will mean starting the selection process in the state where the party is strongest, and working down from there. This way voters in the states where the party is most successful will determine the early results that are the most influential. This sequence will help select the candidates who are the most able to build successfully on the party's past successes, and who are the most able to explain their policies to other potential voters. The schedule that's long and that progresses to states that are increasingly split will give these most-successful candidates more practice refining how they communicate their value proposition in the run-up to the general election. Success breeds success.

Taken together, these party laws will help select the candidates who are best able to maintain the party's brand quality, best able to win, and best able to succeed at representing the people.

An approximate party caucus schedule that's arranged using these party laws is shown in Table 2 below. After that, in Figure 5 below the actual results for the Republican Party in 2016 are shown toward the left, and suggestive results from counting those votes under the laws of the republican Constitution party are shown toward the right.

Table 2. Party caucus schedule and party electoral college applied to 2016 election[59, 60]

The republican Constitution party strengths are approximated as Republican Party strengths. Statewide party strengths are approximated as latest election totals for both senators as of 2014. House district party strengths are approximated as statewide party strengths. District of Columbia total strength is based on election totals for 2014.

Wk	Date	State or district	Party strength	Party electoral college				
				House	Senate	Total	Cumulative	
				n=243	n=53	n=296	Count	%
0	10/27/15	Alabama	76.57%	6	2	8	8	3%
1	11/03/15	Wyoming	74.24%	1	2	3	11	4%
2	11/10/15	South Dakota	72.67%	1	2	3	14	5%
3	11/17/15	Idaho	68.29%	2	2	4	18	6%
4	11/24/15	Oklahoma	67.93%	4	2	6	24	8%
5	12/01/15	Utah	63.86%	4	2	6	30	10%
6	12/08/15	Tennessee	63.77%	7	2	9	39	13%
7	12/15/15	Kansas	61.48%	4	2	6	45	15%
8	12/22/15	North Dakota	60.75%	1	1	2	47	16%
9	12/29/15	Nebraska	60.44%	2	2	4	51	17%
10	01/05/16	Texas	58.35%	25	2	27	78	26%
11	01/12/16	Iowa	58.19%	3	2	5	83	28%
12	01/19/16	Mississippi	58.08%	3	2	5	88	30%
13	01/26/16	South Carolina	57.69%	6	2	8	96	32%
14	02/02/16	Arkansas	57.17%	4	2	6	102	34%
15	02/09/16	Louisiana	56.24%	5	2	7	109	37%
16	02/16/16	Kentucky	55.96%	5	2	7	116	39%
17	02/23/16	Georgia	55.59%	10	2	12	128	43%
18	03/01/16	New Hampshire	53.91%	1	1	2	130	44%
19	03/08/16	Arizona	53.30%	5	2	7	137	46%
20	03/15/16	North Carolina	51.68%	10	2	12	149	50%
21	03/22/16	Montana	50.45%	1	1	2	151	51%
22	03/29/16	Ohio	49.70%	12	1	13	164	55%
23	04/05/16	Maine	49.02%	1	1	2	166	56%

Wk	Date	State or district	Party strength	Party electoral college				
				House	Senate	Total	Cumulative	
				n=243	*n=53*	*n=296*	Count	%
24	04/12/16	Indiana	48.46%	7	1	8	174	59%
25	04/19/16	Wisconsin	48.37%	5	1	6	180	61%
26	04/26/16	Virginia	47.46%	8	–	8	188	64%
27	05/03/16	Colorado	47.36%	4	1	5	193	65%
28	05/10/16	Pennsylvania	47.25%	13	1	14	207	70%
29	05/17/16	West Virginia	46.92%	3	1	4	211	71%
30	05/24/16	Missouri	45.41%	6	1	7	218	74%
31	05/31/16	Illinois	45.39%	8	1	9	227	77%
32	06/07/16	Nevada	45.31%	3	1	4	231	78%
33	06/14/16	New Mexico	44.94%	1	–	1	232	78%
34	06/21/16	Florida	44.88%	14	1	15	247	83%
35	06/28/16	Washington	43.19%	4	–	4	251	85%
36	07/05/16	Connecticut	43.11%	–	–	–	251	85%
37	07/12/16	Massachusetts	42.93%	–	–	–	251	85%
38	07/19/16	Alaska	42.35%	1	1	2	253	85%
39	07/26/16	New Jersey	40.44%	6	–	6	259	88%
40	08/02/16	California	39.56%	14	–	14	273	92%
41	08/09/16	Michigan	39.33%	9	–	9	282	95%
42	08/16/16	Oregon	38.05%	1	–	1	283	96%
43	08/23/16	Minnesota	35.61%	3	–	3	286	97%
44	08/30/16	Delaware	33.86%	–	–	–	286	97%
45	09/06/16	Hawaii	33.02%	–	–	–	286	97%
46	09/13/16	Rhode Island	32.50%	–	–	–	286	97%
47	09/20/16	Maryland	30.20%	1	–	1	287	97%
48	09/27/16	New York	28.73%	9	–	9	296	100%
49	10/04/16	Vermont	28.20%	–	–	–	296	100%
50	10/11/16	District of Columbia	6.79%	–	–	–	296	100%

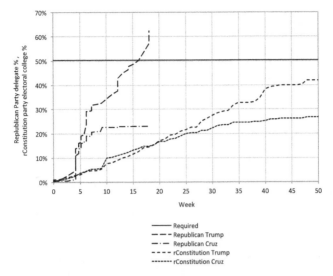

The Republican Party results are actual. The republican Constitution party results are suggestive results from counting those votes under the laws of the republican Constitution party.

Figure 5. Party presidential candidate selection based on 2016 election data[59, 60, 61, 62]

The figure provides results that are suggestive and interesting, but incomplete. It's useful to list each party law requirement, and note the portion of the requirement's effects that the figure doesn't capture:

1. *Conservative Review Liberty Scores of a minimum of 80%*
Some senators either would have voted better in the past, or would have not been in the race.

2. *Moderator-free party-sanctioned debates*

Party-sanctioned debates would have reflected the priorities of the republican Constitution party candidates.

3. *All-closed contests*

All voters would have been republican Constitution party members.

4. *All-caucus contests*

All voters would have been influenced by their best-informed, most-active republican Constitution party neighbors.

5. *All-proportional voting*

Each vote for each candidate in a given state would have had equal influence on voters in later states.

6. *Party electoral college*

Only votes in states that count in the general election would have influenced voters in later states.

7. *Electors only awarded on seats currently held by the party*

Only votes in regions currently represented by the party would have influenced voters in later states.

8. *One-at-a-time contests*

Each vote for each candidate in a given state would have had the same influence on voters in every state that hadn't voted yet.

9. *Contests in order of decreasing party strength*

Each vote in a state would have influenced the voters in every state where the party is less successful.

These omitted effects would have considerably changed the figure's suggestive results. Even so, even under this incomplete implementation of the republican Constitution party laws, Donald Trump already would not have clinched the nomination during the state contests.

The figure vividly illustrates the dramatic upward jumps in delegate percentages under an existing major party's Progressive-favoring rules, contrasted with the much smoother and steadier results under the republican Constitution party laws.

The republican Constitution party laws will provide initial vetting by voters in regions where the party is most successful, which will gradually widen to include vetting by voters in regions where the party has so far been less successful. These party laws are nothing more than the common-sense due diligence that the people in any party would be expected to exercise in conducting the party's affairs, as long as the party has a good brand, and the party people are determined to guard the brand's quality.

Chapter 7

Party's Processes Teach Nation's Processes

GOVERNMENT STRUCTURES under the Constitution are models for the republican Constitution party structures, and this means that the republican Constitution party structures are analogs of the government structures under the Constitution. Given the party's much-smaller scope, having the party as an analog will be very instructive about how to govern properly under the Constitution.

Prior party government structures allow candidate-selection processes to be determined by top-down control. This experience with top-down control helps prepare these parties' elected representatives to legislate and execute Progressive national government that defies the Constitution. Their voters learn from the start to expect to be disappointed.

The republican Constitution party structure will require candidate-selection processes to be determined by exercising separate, offsetting powers within an analog of the government structure provided by the Constitution. This experience of following the party constitution will help prepare this party's elected representatives to legislate and execute constitutional national government by following the Constitution. Their voters will learn from the start to expect to be represented constitutionally.

The republican Constitution party structures in states, counties, and cities would logically follow the same pattern of replicating the structures of separate, offsetting powers that are in their associated governments, so this experience of following party constitutions would help prepare these representatives to work constitutionally within their governments. Voters would learn how to be represented constitutionally. They also would learn how to join in.

People learn most effectively not by memorizing information, but by developing skills at solving problems. Experience is a great teacher. Focus on developing skills, and it turns out that the other information that you need comes along for the ride.[63, 64]

Chapter 8

Party's Firm Boundaries Define Contours of Transition

PRIOR PARTIES' candidate-selection processes leave most voters in general elections with no options to vote for candidates who could win and who would follow the Constitution.

The current elected representatives who follow the Constitution relatively well are unable to get bills passed that follow the Constitution, and are unable to get a majority caucus elected within their prior party that will follow the Constitution.

As mentioned earlier (in the text accompanying Figure 4 above, and in the figure), when change is for the better—as in the former Soviet bloc (which had striking parallels to our one-party

Progressive rule, top-down control, and decreasing freedom)—fast, extensive change produces the results that are the best by far. Fast change helps make sure that larger change is able to take place, because fast change helps overcome the naturally self-interested people who are currently entrenched.[50]

The current elected representatives who follow the Constitution relatively well will have little to lose by joining a new party. If they do not get elected in a given election (which could happen even if they run within their prior party), they are talented people who will do fine in other work, and they can run again later if they choose to.

They have much to gain by joining a new party. When they do get elected, they potentially will start out either with as large a minority caucus as they had previously, or with a larger minority caucus. They will have much-greater upside potential to grow in influence by simply offering good candidates as options for voters all across the ballots in general elections.

Once elected, they will all be ideally prepared to exert outsized influence. Asserting your role boundaries and respecting others' role boundaries offer dramatic improvements in relationships that often have to be experienced to be believed.[65]

The interactions in a relationship involve both partners. Such interactions can seem intractable. How can a dynamic ever change when the dynamic is made up of the separate actions of both partners, and when experience seems to have shown over and over again that the other partner is not going to change (and maybe doesn't even want to change)?

But it turns out that when one partner, by herself, changes, the interactions change and the relationship changes.

In personal relationships, the partners tend to be more-evenly matched.[66] When one partner exerts more power, this makes the other partner change to become more like the stronger partner.[67] If one partner changes to better assert her own role boundaries or to better respect her partner's role boundaries, then her change is good for the relationship, and her partner's resulting change is also good for the relationship. The relationship tends to deepen.

In work life, relationships tend to be more hierarchical. When a paradigm shifts, people who are more invested in the old paradigm tend to continue in the old ways for the rest of their careers. People who are less invested in the old paradigm tend to invest in the new paradigm.[68] The relationships between people who stay invested in the old paradigm and people who invest in the new paradigm tend to break up and tend to grow further estranged over time.

The House Freedom Caucus members and like-minded senators have stood up well to opposition from party leadership and have resiliently won re-elections. Whether within a new party or as members of their prior party, they will naturally propose legislation and vote on legislation less the way that other Republicans do and more the way that like-minded people do. Together, the House Freedom Caucus members and like-minded senators and the republican Constitution party members will be a spontaneously-forming constitutional-conservative caucus.

The new caucus members will hold to their constitutional-conservative boundaries, and Democrats will hold to their Progressive boundaries. The remaining Republicans will find that they can team up with the new caucus members to form majorities, team up with the Democrats to form majorities, or abstain and deadlock.

One plausible outcome would be a fissure along a line determined by people's prior investments of time and effort, with older Republicans mostly teaming up with Democrats, and with younger Republicans mostly teaming up with the new caucus members. Since the new caucus members would hold their boundaries and the Democrats would hold their boundaries, this fissure would mark the remaining Republicans for defeat.

Democrats would be strongly enabled by academics and media who condition voters to favor Democrats' way of positioning their policies, so Democrats would retain their well-established brand as the standard-bearers for nobly-described big government.

Republicans had kept in contention by presenting themselves as the only viable alternative available to voters who want a less in-your-face, smaller, more-constitutional government. But Republicans' monopoly on seeming to be the viable alternative would be broken by the republican Constitution party candidates. Republicans would never be seen as the best party for voters who want big government, and Republicans would no longer seem to be the best party for voters who want small, constitutional government. By standing for nothing firm, Republicans would be the odd men out.

Republicans here and there would manage to hold out for a little while on the strength of strong name recognition and, in some cases, likeability. But as a group—as a party—Republicans, by standing for nothing, would not long stand.

This would turn out to be odd, even a bit tragic, after things play out to their natural conclusion, as described below.

In the prior equilibrium, the Democrats held firmer boundaries, and whatever positions they staked out, the Republicans moved into position right at the margins of these boundaries: they became the Democrat-lite party. But in the new equilibrium of Democrats vs. republican Constitution party people, the republican Constitution party people will have the firmer boundaries by far.

Keep in mind how the Constitution works. The United States of America have long been freer than the European nations, for instance. Freedom produces economic strength. When freedom is maintained, that leads the others in the relationship to move in the direction of more freedom, which is what can be seen to have played out over the many years of the relationships between the USA and the European nations.

Progressivism is statist control, which has no absolute limits. No matter what degree of statist control is attempted, there's always another degree of statist control that's higher, and further degrees of statist control that are higher still. The central control just keeps ratcheting up higher and higher endlessly. You can never make it all the way to infinity. In contrast, a government that protects individual freedom is firmly limited: it stays firmly on the ground. It holds itself back so that it stays within its boundaries.

In a relationship between a fully constitutional party and any other party, the other party will always have weaker boundaries. Even if due to a historical twist of fate the other party turns out to be Democrats who formerly were heavily statist, they will not hold to their former boundaries. Above all, they are opportunists, seeking power of any kind that's available. Given the solidity of the republican Constitution party boundary, the Democrats would move into position just to the left of the margin of this boundary—or if not the Democrats, then some similarly opportunistic successor party—and the surviving competitive party would become the republican Constitution lite party: rConstitution lite.

CHAPTER 9

BUILD TO LAST

THE GOVERNMENT STRUCTURE of offsetting powers created by the Constitution is vulnerable to being bypassed by concerted action by prior parties' people, but it is rugged and able to endure. Even in weakened form it continues to be the best-available government structure in history.

The government's internal structure of offsetting powers, which offers resilience, was mentioned in chapter 2. The government's external supports, which brought success, are worth learning from, to make sure that the recommended party will have analogous external supports.

Earlier in history, agriculture had made it possible to move in large scale into cities, and cities turned out to be local areas that provide highly-valuable network effects.[69] Network effects are what happens whenever people are able to interact more closely, share ideas, learn from each other, and through these interactions generate better ideas faster together. Network effects explain Silicon Valley's strength in electronics, and Houston's strength in petrochemicals.

Later, the Declaration and the Constitution caused kings, dictators, and statist government people to back off, leaving individual free action room to grow, creating the freest big space in history. With the advent of the United States of America, freedom made it possible to work together on a large scale in a large nation, and so freedom in the USA brought highly-valuable network effects to a wide area, the widest in history.

As noted in the previous chapter, as the USA maintained their boundaries, many other nations changed to become more like the USA.

There still was slavery. In the USA, slavery was overcome starting during the presidency of a man claimed as a Progressive hero, Abraham Lincoln,[19] using central control. The people had formed states and had joined the United States to protect the people's sovereign rights, and the people had not given up those rights. Regardless, the new Republicans including Lincoln expanded the national government, empowered the virtually all-white Northern states to push their solution onto the roughly half-white Southern states, imposed lethal top-down control, and destroyed them economically. The Republicans including Lincoln prevented the natural consequence of slavery collapsing on its own from its immorality and from its uncompetitive waste of human potential. And by stoking basic human pushback, the Republicans including Lincoln played an integral and perhaps decisive role in generating the extremely-slow progress in delivering freedom to former slaves that was experienced postwar. Central control by government people is costly and slow. Alternate approaches worked in other nations, and in retrospect may have gotten us to a better place here, without the proto-Progressive government remake.

Later, the USA increasingly became something of a victim of their own success, because they increasingly had the material means to nourish an increasing population of Progressives.

Unseen in most histories of the 1930s, people in business used electrification and factory redesign, and process, material, and transportation advances, to engineer the greatest increase ever seen in total factor productivity: the excess productivity gain above and beyond the productivity gained by adding labor and investing capital—an actual free lunch.[70, 71] But this bountiful harvest, and more, went right out the back door to feed the Progressives.

In these same 1930s, Progressives tried out new, central-control, large-government responses to an ordinarily short-lived steep recession, which is called a depression. Progressives reconstituted World War I top-down control agencies, raised tariffs, pushed for constant wages despite falling prices, raised taxes, broke banks, outlawed gold domestic money, broke up banks, operated make-work programs, interfered with farming, competed with utilities, erected the Social Security Ponzi scheme, promoted union monopolies on labor, promoted price collusion, and more. This full-scale trial and error turned this ordinary depression into the extraordinarily long and devastating Great Depression.[40] FDR's follies[72] and the like have continued to the present day.

Now it's clear that there's a need to overcome the parties' structural flaws. This is an opportunity to again become freer, and to set better boundaries that will lead the world to change for the better again.

The approach that's been described—of reusing a good structure for a new purpose—is basic, common in the world, and well proven.

Scientists, inventors, whole businesses, whole industries innovate by taking proven existing components and combining them in new ways for new uses.[73]

The perception-action controls we use to manipulate objects in the physical world are what we reuse to manipulate symbols in the mental world to perform increasingly-abstract mathematics.[74]

Our perception-action controls themselves have a layered structure in brain tissue, in which each layer of tissue performs similar processing on the information provided by the adjacent layer. In perception, for instance, messages descending through successive layers of tissue are used to make increasingly-detailed predictions of what sensations we will experience. Messages rising back through successive layers of tissue are used to make increasingly-summarized observations of what prediction errors we experienced.[75]

Human social organization has a layered structure too. People interact one-on-one, one-on-one interactions combine in small teams,[76] teams make up plants, plants make up business units, business units make up companies, companies make up industries, industries make up the business sector.

Human government organization has a layered structure as well, with neighborhoods, boroughs, cities, counties, districts, states, nations.

And in these human organizations, at each level, the greatest cooperation and success comes when each subunit asserts its own role boundaries and respects the others' role boundaries. When everyone does his job.

As these examples show, reusing better structures is proven and natural. And in the natural world, the structures that are less fit to survive end up dying out. Businesses die out. Parties die out (although slowly sometimes, when they're fed well by a host nation). Nations die out.

Mounting debt kills nations,[21] even if histories superficially record the causes of death as wars or internal intrigues.

It's far better to end the reign of the prior parties than to stand by and watch the extinguishment of personal freedoms in the nation that has been civilization's greatest hope and model.

Parties in the USA have a track record of living well beyond any justification based on performance. Any new party needs to be designed with the strong possibility in mind that even if the party's design and functioning are quite bad, the party could still survive and be very hard to displace. We could end up having to live with it for a very long time, for better or for worse. So from the start, the party should be built to last.

If the United States of America are to long survive, to thrive, to be a beacon of individual freedom in the world, they must follow the Constitution. The Constitution needs a good party. A good party is built with a structure that robustly resists subversion.

The best-available model for a party is the government under the Declaration and the Constitution.

CHAPTER 10
CATALYSTS FOR PARTY FORMATION

AN ORDINARY CHEMICAL MIXTURE needs lots of energy to get the mixture's atoms close together so they recombine into new products. A catalyst makes it so that less energy is needed to get the mixture's atoms close together so they recombine into new products. (Typically, a catalyst holds onto one of the reactants so another reactant can get close to it more easily.)

Other catalysts make it so that less energy is needed to make changes happen in society. This can make the right changes proceed, and succeed.

The American Revolution came after a multi-decade run-up.

In 1620, people sought religious and economic freedom in America. First, people survived. Then, with taxes never exceeding 1% to 2%, people thrived.[1]

In the 1730s and 1740s, the First Great Awakening prepared people to try to better secure their God-given natural rights.[77]

By 1776, per-capita income purchasing power exceeded that of Great Britain's people by 68%.[2] The king of England had started trying to ratchet up taxes in America so they'd exceed 1% to 2%. People throughout America valued their greater independence and wealth, and they were ready to resist. Resistance was discussed by many people in many places. Revolution was in the air.[3]

Each colony already had an experienced, functioning government. Knowing people's sentiments, their representatives were ready for revolution too.

These sentiments could have led to a revolt that failed, or could have elevated new local rulers, but the representatives found a better path. They had practical experience governing the various colonies, and they were well-educated in practically-applicable political philosophy.[77] The representatives eased the way to self-sustaining, improved government by developing two catalysts:

the 1776 Declaration of Independence; and the 1787 Constitution.

Abolition of slavery came after another multi-decade run-up.

In the 1820s, people experienced the Second Great Awakening. People increasingly supported abolition of slavery.[78]

Since abolition had broad support in large regions of the country, the representatives in those regions also supported abolition.

Ultimately, abolition came about with the help of three catalysts: the 1854 Kansas-Nebraska Act allowing slavery in the North; the 1854 formation of the Republican Party; and the 1861 Confederate States' secession and attack on Fort Sumter.

(Escalation to industrial-scale war might have been avoided by peacefully implementing the existing 5th-Amendment protection of liberty. Or, by peacefully first allowing secession and then implementing the existing 5th-Amendment protection of liberty before states reentered the Union.

Slavery not only was repugnant, but also was a great waste of human potential. As a result, from 1774 to 1860 the fraction of total personal income in all thirteen colonies or states that was earned in the slavery-is-legal region declined from 57% to 31%.[79]

Slavery and discrimination were ended incompletely by the war and the resulting impoverishment. Slavery and discrimination might well have ended much more completely and rapidly by peace, with continuing increases in prosperity.

This could have happened in multiple ways at once. The slaveholding regions were falling behind. When people fall behind, they learn from others—for instance, from others in the freer regions—and they change. At the same time, the slaveholding regions also were slowly but steadily growing more prosperous. When people get prosperous enough, they dramatically clean up themselves and their neighborhoods.[80,81,82])

A return to more-constitutional government isn't as far along yet as the decades from the First Great Awakening to the American Revolution, and from the Second Great Awakening to abolition.

In 2009, the rise of Tea Party activism was the first large-scale movement toward returning to more-constitutional government. Despite this, we currently have uncertain support among the public for returning to more-constitutional government by breaking away from the current parties.

More-constitutional representatives have stepped up, have overcome the many barriers put up by the Republican Party people and by media people, and have won election and reelection. Despite this, we currently have too few of these representatives. We currently have uncertain understanding among these representatives that our individual rights are secured only when government people fully use their constitutional powers against other government people. And we currently have uncertain support among these representatives for returning to more-constitutional government by breaking away from the current parties.

In 2016, voters chose Donald Trump as the presidential candidate who they thought would bring the most-decisive change toward constitutional small government.

Since then, a return to more-constitutional government has been further encouraged by still more potentially-precipitating events: betrayal on Obamacare repeal; and record-high spending. Both were epic fails from the best-available major party for people who support constitutional small government.

For voters interested in more-constitutional government, it would take lots of energy to confidently vote for a new party. Most voters would want to be able to reasonably anticipate that the new party's candidates could be elected.

For activists interested in more-constitutional government, it would take lots of energy to help form a new party and help the party win elections. Nearly all activists are currently focusing their efforts on activities that won't help create a new party that's robustly designed to keep selecting more-constitutional candidates.

For the more-constitutional current representatives, it would take lots of energy to form or to help form a new party, and to win their first elections in the new party. Rather than just winning again in primaries and then in general-election matchups that are one-on-one, they'd have to win general-election matchups that are one against two: against both a Democrat and a Republican.

A new party can be pushed along by popular sentiment, or pulled along by a small group of currently-elected representatives, or both.

But so far we have too little to show for various people's efforts. Despite voter interest, Tea Party energy, and some more-constitutional elected representatives, so far voters, activists, and representatives aren't very close to being all on the same page. As a starting point for action, people need a shared understanding and a framework for action.

Voters, activists, and representatives could get more-constitutional government more surely and more quickly if they had good catalysts.

One catalyst could be *The Constitution Needs a Good Party*.

This book can raise awareness in the public, among activists, and in the more-constitutional current representatives that constitutional government actually involves not the current Kabuki-theatre play-fighting, but real ongoing conflicts ("constitutional crises"), in which government people vigorously exercise their many barely-used constitutional powers against other government people.

This book also can raise awareness of how a party can be designed to be much better than prior parties at resisting being compromised by future party people.

Learning from the proven example of how the nation's name, the Declaration of Independence, and the Constitution created a distinctly-improved government, this book advocates a party name, party declaration, party constitution, and party laws that would create a distinctly-improved party.

And an improved party is what's needed to return to that improved constitutional government.

Another catalyst could be republican Constitution party organizing meetings.

Overall, the goal of these meetings should be to help a good new party form not after a multi-decade run-up but instead in mere years, by proceeding with upfront legwork that will reduce the energy needed for further action.

The goal of these meetings should explicitly not be to form the actual party. Nothing could discourage interest like an unimpressive start in a national election or in a state election.

Also, these meetings should not discourage current representatives from secretly forming the republican Constitution party. Rather, these meetings should encourage current representatives to either secretly form, or openly join in forming, the republican Constitution party.

One starting point for party-organizing meetings could be informal discussions in meetings of all kinds of existing groups: friends and neighbors could discuss the republican Constitution party when they get together; current activist-group members could discuss the republican Constitution party at their meetings; prayer-group members could mention the republican Constitution party in side conversations.

Ideally, each group hosting party-organizing meetings would start by endorsing using the framework in *The Constitution Needs a Good Party* as the framework for a new party.

Beyond that, party-organizing meetings could be refined to increasingly resemble the future party's caucuses, and to begin developing the infrastructure to run the future party's candidate-selection process. If you build it, they will come.[83]

These meetings would help begin developing several essentials:

1. *Party commitment*

The future party would select candidates using caucuses that are open only to party members.

Before the future party was formed, commitment to the party would be nonexclusive. But early commitment and participation would strongly indicate to prospective candidates that the party, once formed, would have the necessary votes.

And it's votes, not dollars, that win elections.

2. *Party interest*

Meetings, future caucuses, and the developing presidential candidate-selection races as caucuses proceed would attract interested voters, and would increase party turnout in general elections.

3. *Caucus schedule*

Caucuses would be used to select candidates for all levels of government. Caucuses to select presidential candidates would be sequenced to take place first in the state where the party is strongest, next in the state where the party is next strongest, and so on.

Before the future party was formed, party-organizing meetings would similarly be scheduled to prepare voters for all elections. Meetings would immediately precede the current parties' primaries or caucuses, and the general elections.

That would be the extent of the time called for. Supervision of government, while important, needs to be put in its proper place. If we the people are really sovereign, then we're really in control of our own lives. That means that our supervision of government must be doable as a convenient, part-time activity.

4. *Caucus venues*

In 2016, the total number of general election voters was about 137 million.[84] A winning majority would be about 68 million. If all these voters turned out for caucuses (since interest could be very high), and if each caucus was attended by 25 party members, then the number of caucuses needed would be about 2.7 million.

The people are sovereign, not the government. The sovereign people have their own assets, and aren't dependent on governments. To avoid furthering the harmful impression that various current government-controlled approaches like government-monopoly schools are the only way or the best way, caucus hosts should only use venues that are not connected with governments: homes, businesses, private schools, churches, and other organizations not funded by governments.

5. *Caucus experience*

Caucuses would address a real need in our politics for community. Unlike solitary, impersonal voting, a caucus would be an inviting, shared community experience.

Caucuses, and caucus hosts, would attract people to the party, and to voting in general elections.

People would go to whichever caucus they'd like to go to. If attendance was high at a given venue, people could quickly spin off a new caucus and meet elsewhere.

Caucuses would have no set durations. Like baseball innings and baseball games, caucuses would be as short or as long as needed on game day.

Caucuses would not develop party platforms, since each candidate would be solely responsible for his own policy positions. Caucuses would select party officials, but these selections would have limited impact since the party wouldn't fund campaigns. Caucuses would chiefly help party members select candidates.

To help party members select candidates, caucuses would help people share information. The people who have the best data would have the most impact.[85]

Caucus hosts would plan to host a full caucus of around 25 party members, with small-group breakout meetings of around 5 party members.

In each caucus, the small groups would exchange information, the full caucus would exchange information, and the party members who attended would then be authorized to vote in the caucus.

6. *Caucus voting*

Once the party members who had attended a caucus were authorized to vote in the caucus, the party members could use their own computers or mobile devices to cast their caucus votes.

7. *Party-government operation*

National-party legislators and state-party legislators would review existing party laws to make sure that each law is helping to ensure brand quality. Conservative Review Liberty Scores would initially be used to qualify national candidates. Additional rankings could be used to qualify state candidates.[86] Development of rankings for state candidates by private organizations would be catalyzed by the party-organizing meetings and then by the caucuses.

Party senators would advise and consent on schedules for party-sanctioned debates.

National and state party executives would maintain basic organization data on the web:

- Party declaration of independence
- Party constitutions, national and state
- Party laws, national and state
- Party officers' contact info
- Party calendars that show addresses of local caucuses
- Party-voting pages

Development of this web infrastructure would also be catalyzed by the party-organizing meetings.

When a new party was ultimately launched, its design would benefit from contributions from people with varied and complementary backgrounds and expertise.

Elected representatives have detailed knowledge of how to win elections in a hostile environment, and of how to represent voters in a hostile environment.

Prospective candidates have some of the same knowledge, are willing to take calculated risks, and have the stamina to build name recognition across multiple candidacies as-needed.

Activists have energy, knowledge, and existing networks. Even activists currently in other minority parties and organizations could decide that their interests would be served very well by supporting a new major party that provides more-constitutional government.

Such a government would in part use federalism to remove from the national government the many contentious policy issues that aren't within the scope of the national government's enumerated powers, and to move these issues to where they constitutionally belong, in the states. As in the individual colonies and in the individual states originally, the state-government people would once again try out a variety of approaches in the various policy areas that are constitutionally within the scope of the state governments. People in each state would be able to move to different states whose government people's approaches suit them better. State-government people would have strong incentives to keep their current people and to attract new people, so state-government people would be quicker to learn what works well elsewhere and develop new approaches to better suit their people. Given more freedom in each state, people nationwide would have more freedom in more policy areas.[4]

To stay strong and to achieve shared goals, disparate groups may choose to join together, just like the American Colonies needed to join together, as dramatized in Figure 6. This wood-cut was made by Ben Franklin in 1754, a full two decades before the American Revolutionary War started in 1775.

Figure 6. JOIN, or DIE.[87]

In our change to more-constitutional government, the rate-limiting step is widespread diffusion of a deeper understanding of just how different our national, state, and local governments could be. When there's a big difference between where things are and where things could be, and when most people agree about this, this difference is a strong driving force for change.

What paths are ultimately taken will depend on the skills and the actions of the individuals who wind up making the changes. The paths taken and the timing will also depend on further galvanizing events that have yet to be seen.

For the American Revolution, first John Locke set out ideas on natural rights and separation of powers. Then, in time, people and representatives became ready for war and ready to form a new government.[77] The king of England helped finalize the timing.

People are more disposed to suffer, while evils are sufferable, than to right themselves by abolishing the forms of government to which they are accustomed.[88] But over time, the strong desire for freedom brought the ideas that were needed to secure freedom, and then brought the people who were needed to secure freedom.

Here and now, this freedom can be made more secure much faster.

Chapter 11

First Steps
for Individuals

YOU MAY BE THINKING that this information is good, but we don't have a well-designed party yet, so what can we do right now as individuals?

One thing that, for me, really helps is to be very selective about reading and other information sources.

I pay careful attention to how commentators view current events, comparing the commentators' expectations with my expectations of how people would act if they followed the Constitution well. What constitutional powers are various government people failing to use against each other? If Progressives reach across the aisle and act in a bipartisan manner, what would that do to my life, liberty, and property?

Talk from people in government nearly always is a major distraction. People in government have the power and duty to act, so I focus on their actions and inactions. What are the president and the governors actively managing, and what are they passively leaving on autopilot? What are the Congress people and the state legislators actively legislating, and what are they passively leaving in place?

Actions are just policymaking in motion. So naturally I seek commentators who focus on policy.

I also appreciate people who offer data: data about businesses where people add value; data about economic history; scientific observations.

Finding even one or two commentators who think for the long term helps me feel not alone, and much more hopeful.

A second thing that really helps is to simply vote for the best candidates.

I know that it's not my job to second-guess how everyone else is going to vote and what might happen. It helps that I know that if a Progressive wins, nothing substantive will improve, so there's little point in choosing a Progressive Republican over a Progressive Democrat. My votes are not intended to control what happens. My votes are not intended to send a message to Progressives. Progressives aren't listening, and they aren't going to change their spots and provide me the policies I would choose. I just pick the most-constitutional candidates.

My votes show what I stand for. For people who are deciding whether to run for office, and and who if elected would use their constitutional powers, votes like mine provide solid data about how many people are ready to vote for them. My votes are incentives.

In Republican primaries, for now, picking the most-constitutional candidates can really matter. In general elections, it may take a short time or a longer time for suitable candidates to get on ballots, but we voters can at least be ready.

I do the right thing and let the chips fall where they may.

A third thing that really helps is to connect with others and to communicate about the subjects of this book. I talk with people I know; I write to people I don't know.

If you've read this far, you likely already influence the people you know, and now you likely will influence the people you know even more.

One way you can also influence people you don't know is to write a review of this book. Anywhere will do. This is true even in places where many people have provided reviews already. Mention something you liked, mention something you didn't like. Say what you found surprising or useful. Above all, give people data to work with. Help people decide whether they want to check out this book themselves and find out what they think of it themselves. Many people already feel in their gut the way we feel.

If more people read this book, more people will have this book's commonsense understanding of how the Constitution is designed to work, what we're missing out on, and how quickly everything can change for the better.

Our representatives can achieve so much better for us, and not by any means just at the national level.

In state offices, all representatives and judges take an oath to uphold the Constitution.[37] And all powers that are not delegated to the national government by the Constitution, and that are not prohibited to the states by the Constitution, are reserved to the states or to the people.[54] Almost all the powers that are being unconstitutionally exercised against us are legally—constitutionally—the powers of the state government people. Once their eyes are opened, once they're empowered by voters, they'll find low-hanging fruit in every direction they look.

Everywhere, always, good government comes from good boundaries.

Part 2

USA Constitution[89, 90, 91, 92]

We the People of the United States, in Order to form a more perfect Union, establish Justice, insure domestic Tranquility, provide for the common defence, promote the general Welfare, and secure the Blessings of Liberty to ourselves and our Posterity, do ordain and establish this Constitution for the United States of America.

ARTICLE I

LEGISLATIVE

Section 1

All legislative Powers herein granted shall be vested in a Congress of the United States, which shall consist of a Senate and House of Representatives.

Section 2

[1] The House of Representatives shall be composed of Members chosen every second Year by the People of the several States, and the Electors in each State shall have the Qualifications requisite for Electors of the most numerous Branch of the State Legislature.

[2] No Person shall be a Representative who shall not have attained to the Age of twenty five

Years, and been seven Years a Citizen of the United States, and who shall not, when elected, be an Inhabitant of that State in which he shall be chosen.

³ Representatives and direct Taxes shall be apportioned among the several States which may be included within this Union, according to their respective Numbers, which shall be determined by adding to the whole Number of free Persons, including those bound to Service for a Term of Years, and excluding Indians not taxed, three fifths of all other Persons.[a] The actual Enumeration shall be made within three Years after the first Meeting of the Congress of the United States, and within every subsequent Term of ten Years, in such Manner as they shall by Law direct. The Number of Representatives shall not exceed one for every thirty Thousand, but each State shall have at Least one Representative; and until such enumeration shall be made, the State of New Hampshire shall be entitled to chuse three, Massachusetts eight, Rhode-Island and Providence Plantations one, Connecticut five, New-York six, New Jersey four,

---

[a] The part of this clause relating to the mode of apportionment of representatives among the several States has been affected by section 2 of Amendment 14, and as to taxes on incomes without apportionment by Amendment 16.

Pennsylvania eight, Delaware one, Maryland six, Virginia ten, North Carolina five, South Carolina five, and Georgia three.

[4] When vacancies happen in the Representation from any State, the Executive Authority thereof shall issue Writs of Election to fill such Vacancies.

[5] The House of Representatives shall chuse their Speaker and other Officers; and shall have the sole Power of Impeachment.

Section 3

[1] The Senate of the United States shall be composed of two Senators from each State, chosen by the Legislature thereof,[b] for six Years; and each Senator shall have one Vote.

[2] Immediately after they shall be assembled in Consequence of the first Election, they shall be divided as equally as may be into three Classes. The Seats of the Senators of the first Class shall be vacated at the Expiration of the second Year, of the second Class at the Expiration of the fourth Year, and of the third Class at the Expiration of the sixth Year, so that one third may be chosen every second Year; and if Vacancies happen by Resignation, or otherwise, during the Recess of

---

[b] This clause has been affected by clause 1 of Amendment 17.

the Legislature of any State, the Executive thereof may make temporary Appointments until the next Meeting of the Legislature, which shall then fill such Vacancies.

[3] No Person shall be a Senator who shall not have attained to the Age of thirty Years, and been nine Years a Citizen of the United States, and who shall not, when elected, be an Inhabitant of that State for which he shall be chosen.[c]

[4] The Vice President of the United States shall be President of the Senate, but shall have no Vote, unless they be equally divided.

[5] The Senate shall chuse their other Officers, and also a President pro tempore, in the Absence of the Vice President, or when he shall exercise the Office of President of the United States.

[6] The Senate shall have the sole Power to try all Impeachments. When sitting for that Purpose, they shall be on Oath or Affirmation. When the President of the United States is tried, the Chief Justice shall preside: And no Person shall be convicted without the Concurrence of two thirds of the Members present.

[7] Judgment in Cases of Impeachment shall not extend further than to removal from Office,

---

[c] This clause has been affected by clause 2 of Amendment 18.

and disqualification to hold and enjoy any Office of honor, Trust or Profit under the United States: but the Party convicted shall nevertheless be liable and subject to Indictment, Trial, Judgment and Punishment, according to Law.

Section 4

[1] The Times, Places and Manner of holding Elections for Senators and Representatives, shall be prescribed in each State by the Legislature thereof; but the Congress may at any time by Law make or alter such Regulations, except as to the Places of chusing Senators.

[2] The Congress shall assemble at least once in every Year, and such Meeting shall be on the first Monday in December,[d] unless they shall by Law appoint a different Day.

Section 5

[1] Each House shall be the Judge of the Elections, Returns and Qualifications of its own Members, and a Majority of each shall constitute a Quorum to do Business; but a smaller Number may adjourn from day to day, and may be authorized to compel the Attendance of absent Members, in

---

[d] This clause has been affected by Amendment 20.

such Manner, and under such Penalties as each House may provide.

² Each House may determine the Rules of its Proceedings, punish its Members for disorderly Behaviour, and, with the Concurrence of two thirds, expel a Member.

³ Each House shall keep a Journal of its Proceedings, and from time to time publish the same, excepting such Parts as may in their Judgment require Secrecy; and the Yeas and Nays of the Members of either House on any question shall, at the Desire of one fifth of those Present, be entered on the Journal.

⁴ Neither House, during the Session of Congress, shall, without the Consent of the other, adjourn for more than three days, nor to any other Place than that in which the two Houses shall be sitting.

Section 6

¹ The Senators and Representatives shall receive a Compensation for their Services, to be ascertained by Law, and paid out of the Treasury of the United States.ᵉ They shall in all Cases, except Treason, Felony and Breach of the Peace,

---

ᵉ This clause has been affected by Amendment 27.

be privileged from Arrest during their Attendance at the Session of their respective Houses, and in going to and returning from the same; and for any Speech or Debate in either House, they shall not be questioned in any other Place.

[2] No Senator or Representative shall, during the Time for which he was elected, be appointed to any civil Office under the Authority of the United States, which shall have been created, or the Emoluments whereof shall have been encreased during such time; and no Person holding any Office under the United States, shall be a Member of either House during his Continuance in Office.

Section 7

[1] All Bills for raising Revenue shall originate in the House of Representatives; but the Senate may propose or concur with Amendments as on other Bills.

[2] Every Bill which shall have passed the House of Representatives and the Senate, shall, before it become a Law, be presented to the President of the United States; If he approve he shall sign it, but if not he shall return it, with his Objections to that House in which it shall have originated, who shall enter the Objections at large on their Journal, and proceed to reconsider it.

If after such Reconsideration two thirds of that House shall agree to pass the Bill, it shall be sent, together with the Objections, to the other House, by which it shall likewise be reconsidered, and if approved by two thirds of that House, it shall become a Law. But in all such Cases the Votes of both Houses shall be determined by yeas and Nays, and the Names of the Persons voting for and against the Bill shall be entered on the Journal of each House respectively. If any Bill shall not be returned by the President within ten Days (Sundays excepted) after it shall have been presented to him, the Same shall be a Law, in like Manner as if he had signed it, unless the Congress by their Adjournment prevent its Return, in which Case it shall not be a Law.

[3] Every Order, Resolution, or Vote to which the Concurrence of the Senate and House of Representatives may be necessary (except on a question of Adjournment) shall be presented to the President of the United States; and before the Same shall take Effect, shall be approved by him, or being disapproved by him, shall be repassed by two thirds of the Senate and House of Representatives, according to the Rules and Limitations prescribed in the Case of a Bill.

Section 8

¹ The Congress shall have Power To lay and collect Taxes, Duties, Imposts and Excises, to pay the Debts and provide for the common Defence and general Welfare of the United States; but all Duties, Imposts and Excises shall be uniform throughout the United States;

² To borrow Money on the credit of the United States;

³ To regulate Commerce with foreign Nations, and among the several States, and with the Indian Tribes;

⁴ To establish an uniform Rule of Naturalization, and uniform Laws on the subject of Bankruptcies throughout the United States;

⁵ To coin Money, regulate the Value thereof, and of foreign Coin, and fix the Standard of Weights and Measures;

⁶ To provide for the Punishment of counterfeiting the Securities and current Coin of the United States;

⁷ To establish Post Offices and post Roads;

⁸ To promote the Progress of Science and useful Arts, by securing for limited Times to Authors and Inventors the exclusive Right to their respective Writings and Discoveries;

[9] To constitute Tribunals inferior to the supreme Court;

[10] To define and punish Piracies and Felonies committed on the high Seas, and Offences against the Law of Nations;

[11] To declare War, grant Letters of Marque and Reprisal, and make Rules concerning Captures on Land and Water;

[12] To raise and support Armies, but no Appropriation of Money to that Use shall be for a longer Term than two Years;

[13] To provide and maintain a Navy;

[14] To make Rules for the Government and Regulation of the land and naval Forces;

[15] To provide for calling forth the Militia to execute the Laws of the Union, suppress Insurrections and repel Invasions;

[16] To provide for organizing, arming, and disciplining, the Militia, and for governing such Part of them as may be employed in the Service of the United States, reserving to the States respectively, the Appointment of the Officers, and the Authority of training the Militia according to the discipline prescribed by Congress;

[17] To exercise exclusive Legislation in all Cases whatsoever, over such District (not exceeding ten Miles square) as may, by Cession of particular

States, and the Acceptance of Congress, become the Seat of the Government of the United States, and to exercise like Authority over all Places purchased by the Consent of the Legislature of the State in which the Same shall be, for the Erection of Forts, Magazines, Arsenals, dock-Yards, and other needful Buildings; — And

[18] To make all Laws which shall be necessary and proper for carrying into Execution the foregoing Powers, and all other Powers vested by this Constitution in the Government of the United States, or in any Department or Officer thereof.

Section 9

[1] The Migration or Importation of such Persons as any of the States now existing shall think proper to admit, shall not be prohibited by the Congress prior to the Year one thousand eight hundred and eight, but a Tax or duty may be imposed on such Importation, not exceeding ten dollars for each Person.

[2] The Privilege of the Writ of Habeas Corpus shall not be suspended, unless when in Cases of Rebellion or Invasion the public Safety may require it.

[3] No Bill of Attainder or ex post facto Law shall be passed.

[4] No Capitation, or other direct, Tax shall be laid, unless in Proportion to the Census or enumeration herein before directed to be taken.[f]

[5] No Tax or Duty shall be laid on Articles exported from any State.

[6] No Preference shall be given by any Regulation of Commerce or Revenue to the Ports of one State over those of another: nor shall Vessels bound to, or from, one State, be obliged to enter, clear, or pay Duties in another.

[7] No Money shall be drawn from the Treasury, but in Consequence of Appropriations made by Law; and a regular Statement and Account of the Receipts and Expenditures of all public Money shall be published from time to time.

[8] No Title of Nobility shall be granted by the United States: And no Person holding any Office of Profit or Trust under them, shall, without the Consent of the Congress, accept of any present, Emolument, Office, or Title, of any kind whatever, from any King, Prince, or foreign State.

Section 10

[1] No State shall enter into any Treaty, Alliance, or Confederation; grant Letters of Marque and

---

[f] This clause has been affected by Amendment 16.

Reprisal; coin Money; emit Bills of Credit; make any Thing but gold and silver Coin a Tender in Payment of Debts; pass any Bill of Attainder, ex post facto Law, or Law impairing the Obligation of Contracts, or grant any Title of Nobility.

[2] No State shall, without the Consent of the Congress, lay any Imposts or Duties on Imports or Exports, except what may be absolutely necessary for executing it's inspection Laws: and the net Produce of all Duties and Imposts, laid by any State on Imports or Exports, shall be for the Use of the Treasury of the United States; and all such Laws shall be subject to the Revision and Controul of the Congress.

[3] No State shall, without the Consent of Congress, lay any Duty of Tonnage, keep Troops, or Ships of War in time of Peace, enter into any Agreement or Compact with another State, or with a foreign Power, or engage in War, unless actually invaded, or in such imminent Danger as will not admit of delay.

Article II

Executive

Section 1

[1] The executive Power shall be vested in a President of the United States of America. He shall hold his Office during the Term of four Years, and, together with the Vice President, chosen for the same Term, be elected, as follows

[2] Each State shall appoint, in such Manner as the Legislature thereof may direct, a Number of Electors, equal to the whole Number of Senators and Representatives to which the State may be entitled in the Congress: but no Senator or Representative, or Person holding an Office of Trust or Profit under the United States, shall be appointed an Elector.

[3] The Electors shall meet in their respective States, and vote by Ballot for two Persons, of whom one at least shall not be an Inhabitant of the same State with themselves. And they shall make a List of all the Persons voted for, and of the Number of Votes for each; which List they shall sign and certify, and transmit sealed to the Seat of the Government of the United States, directed to the President of the Senate. The President of the Senate shall, in the Presence of the Senate and House of Representatives, open all the Certificates, and the Votes shall then be counted. The Person having the greatest Number of Votes shall be the President, if such Number be a Majority of the whole Number of Electors appointed; and if there be more than one who have such Majority, and have an equal Number of Votes, then the House of Representatives shall immediately chuse by Ballot one of them for President; and if no Person have a Majority, then from the five highest on the List the said House shall in like Manner chuse the President. But in chusing the President, the Votes shall be taken by States, the Representation from each State having one Vote; A quorum for this Purpose shall consist of a Member or Members from two thirds of the States, and a Majority of all the States shall be necessary to a Choice. In

every Case, after the Choice of the President, the Person having the greatest Number of Votes of the Electors shall be the Vice President. But if there should remain two or more who have equal Votes, the Senate shall chuse from them by Ballot the Vice President.[g]

[4] The Congress may determine the Time of chusing the Electors, and the Day on which they shall give their Votes; which Day shall be the same throughout the United States.

[5] No Person except a natural born Citizen, or a Citizen of the United States, at the time of the Adoption of this Constitution, shall be eligible to the Office of President; neither shall any Person be eligible to that Office who shall not have attained to the Age of thirty five Years, and been fourteen Years a Resident within the United States.

[6] In Case of the Removal of the President from Office, or of his Death, Resignation, or Inability to discharge the Powers and Duties of the said Office,[h] the Same shall devolve on the Vice President, and the Congress may by Law provide for the Case of Removal, Death, Resignation or Inability, both of the President and Vice President, declaring what Officer shall then act as President,

---

[g] This clause has been superseded by Amendment 12.

[h] This clause has been affected by Amendment 25.

and such Officer shall act accordingly, until the Disability be removed, or a President shall be elected.

[7] The President shall, at stated Times, receive for his Services, a Compensation, which shall neither be encreased nor diminished during the Period for which he shall have been elected, and he shall not receive within that Period any other Emolument from the United States, or any of them.

[8] Before he enter on the Execution of his Office, he shall take the following Oath or Affirmation: —" I do solemnly swear (or affirm) that I will faithfully execute the Office of President of the United States, and will to the best of my Ability, preserve, protect and defend the Constitution of the United States."

Section 2

[1] The President shall be Commander in Chief of the Army and Navy of the United States, and of the Militia of the several States, when called into the actual Service of the United States; he may require the Opinion, in writing, of the principal Officer in each of the executive Departments, upon any Subject relating to the Duties of their respective Offices, and he shall have Power to grant

Reprieves and Pardons for Offences against the United States, except in Cases of Impeachment.

[2] He shall have Power, by and with the Advice and Consent of the Senate, to make Treaties, provided two thirds of the Senators present concur; and he shall nominate, and by and with the Advice and Consent of the Senate, shall appoint Ambassadors, other public Ministers and Consuls, Judges of the supreme Court, and all other Officers of the United States, whose Appointments are not herein otherwise provided for, and which shall be established by Law: but the Congress may by Law vest the Appointment of such inferior Officers, as they think proper, in the President alone, in the Courts of Law, or in the Heads of Departments.

[3] The President shall have Power to fill up all Vacancies that may happen during the Recess of the Senate, by granting Commissions which shall expire at the End of their next Session.

Section 3

He shall from time to time give to the Congress Information of the State of the Union, and recommend to their Consideration such Measures as he shall judge necessary and expedient; he may, on extraordinary Occasions, convene both Houses, or either of them, and in Case of

Disagreement between them, with Respect to the Time of Adjournment, he may adjourn them to such Time as he shall think proper; he shall receive Ambassadors and other public Ministers; he shall take Care that the Laws be faithfully executed, and shall Commission all the Officers of the United States.

Section 4

The President, Vice President and all civil Officers of the United States, shall be removed from Office on Impeachment for, and Conviction of, Treason, Bribery, or other high Crimes and Misdemeanors.

ARTICLE III

JUDICIAL

Section 1

The judicial Power of the United States, shall be vested in one supreme Court, and in such inferior Courts as the Congress may from time to time ordain and establish. The Judges, both of the supreme and inferior Courts, shall hold their Offices during good Behaviour, and shall, at stated Times, receive for their Services, a Compensation, which shall not be diminished during their Continuance in Office.

Section 2

[1] The judicial Power shall extend to all Cases, in Law and Equity, arising under this Constitution, the Laws of the United States, and Treaties made,

or which shall be made, under their Authority; — to all Cases affecting Ambassadors, other public Ministers and Consuls; — to all Cases of admiralty and maritime Jurisdiction; — to Controversies to which the United States shall be a Party; — to Controversies between two or more States; — between a State and Citizens of another State,[i] — between Citizens of different States, — between Citizens of the same State claiming Lands under Grants of different States, and between a State, or the Citizens thereof, and foreign States, Citizens or Subjects.

[2] In all Cases affecting Ambassadors, other public Ministers and Consuls, and those in which a State shall be Party, the supreme Court shall have original Jurisdiction. In all the other Cases before mentioned, the supreme Court shall have appellate Jurisdiction, both as to Law and Fact, with such Exceptions, and under such Regulations as the Congress shall make.

[3] The Trial of all Crimes, except in Cases of Impeachment, shall be by Jury; and such Trial shall be held in the State where the said Crimes shall have been committed; but when not committed within any State, the Trial shall be at such

---

i This clause has been affected by Amendment 11.

Place or Places as the Congress may by Law have directed.

Section 3

[1] Treason against the United States, shall consist only in levying War against them, or in adhering to their Enemies, giving them Aid and Comfort. No Person shall be convicted of Treason unless on the Testimony of two Witnesses to the same overt Act, or on Confession in open Court.

[2] The Congress shall have Power to declare the Punishment of Treason, but no Attainder of Treason shall work Corruption of Blood, or Forfeiture except during the Life of the Person attainted.

ARTICLE IV

STATES

Section 1
Full Faith and Credit shall be given in each State to the public Acts, Records, and judicial Proceedings of every other State. And the Congress may by general Laws prescribe the Manner in which such Acts, Records and Proceedings shall be proved, and the Effect thereof.

Section 2
[1] The Citizens of each State shall be entitled to all Privileges and Immunities of Citizens in the several States.

[2] A Person charged in any State with Treason, Felony, or other Crime, who shall flee from Justice, and be found in another State, shall on Demand

of the executive Authority of the State from which he fled, be delivered up, to be removed to the State having Jurisdiction of the Crime.

[3] No Person held to Service or Labour in one State, under the Laws thereof, escaping into another, shall, in Consequence of any Law or Regulation therein, be discharged from such Service or Labour, but shall be delivered up on Claim of the Party to whom such Service or Labour may be due.[j]

Section 3

[1] New States may be admitted by the Congress into this Union; but no new State shall be formed or erected within the Jurisdiction of any other State; nor any State be formed by the Junction of two or more States, or Parts of States, without the Consent of the Legislatures of the States concerned as well as of the Congress.

[2] The Congress shall have Power to dispose of and make all needful Rules and Regulations respecting the Territory or other Property belonging to the United States; and nothing in this Constitution shall be so construed as to Prejudice

---

j   This clause has been affected by Amendment 13.

any Claims of the United States, or of any particular State.

Section 4

The United States shall guarantee to every State in this Union a Republican Form of Government, and shall protect each of them against Invasion; and on Application of the Legislature, or of the Executive (when the Legislature cannot be convened), against domestic Violence.

ARTICLE V

AMENDMENT

THE CONGRESS, WHENEVER two thirds of both Houses shall deem it necessary, shall propose Amendments to this Constitution, or, on the Application of the Legislatures of two thirds of the several States, shall call a Convention for proposing Amendments, which, in either Case, shall be valid to all Intents and Purposes, as Part of this Constitution, when ratified by the Legislatures of three fourths of the several States, or by Conventions in three fourths thereof, as the one or the other Mode of Ratification may be proposed by the Congress; Provided that no Amendment which may be made prior to the Year One thousand eight hundred and eight shall in any Manner affect the first and fourth Clauses in the Ninth Section of the first Article; and that no State, without its Consent, shall be deprived of its equal Suffrage in the Senate.

ARTICLE VI

SUPREME-LAW SUPPORT

[1] All Debts contracted and Engagements entered into, before the Adoption of this Constitution, shall be as valid against the United States under this Constitution, as under the Confederation.

[2] This Constitution, and the Laws of the United States which shall be made in Pursuance thereof; and all Treaties made, or which shall be made, under the Authority of the United States, shall be the supreme Law of the Land; and the Judges in every State shall be bound thereby, any Thing in the Constitution or Laws of any State to the Contrary notwithstanding.

[3] The Senators and Representatives before mentioned, and the Members of the several State Legislatures, and all executive and judicial

Officers, both of the United States and of the several States, shall be bound by Oath or Affirmation, to support this Constitution; but no religious Test shall ever be required as a Qualification to any Office or public Trust under the United States.

ARTICLE VII

RATIFICATION

THE RATIFICATION OF THE Conventions of nine States, shall be sufficient for the Establishment of this Constitution between the States so ratifying the Same.

AMENDMENT 1

RELIGION AND SPEECH

CONGRESS SHALL MAKE no law respecting an establishment of religion, or prohibiting the free exercise thereof; or abridging the freedom of speech, or of the press; or the right of the people peaceably to assemble, and to petition the Government for a redress of grievances.

Amendment 2

Arms

A WELL REGULATED MILITIA, being necessary to the security of a free State, the right of the people to keep and bear Arms, shall not be infringed.

Amendment 3

Quartering

No Soldier shall, in time of peace be quartered in any house, without the consent of the Owner, nor in time of war, but in a manner to be prescribed by law.

Amendment 4
Searches and Seizures

THE RIGHT OF THE PEOPLE to be secure in their persons, houses, papers, and effects, against unreasonable searches and seizures, shall not be violated, and no Warrants shall issue, but upon probable cause, supported by Oath or affirmation, and particularly describing the place to be searched, and the persons or things to be seized.

AMENDMENT 5

LIFE, LIBERTY, AND PROPERTY

No PERSON SHALL BE held to answer for a capital, or otherwise infamous crime, unless on a presentment or indictment of a Grand Jury, except in cases arising in the land or naval forces, or in the Militia, when in actual service in time of War or public danger; nor shall any person be subject for the same offence to be twice put in jeopardy of life or limb; nor shall be compelled in any criminal case to be a witness against himself, nor be deprived of life, liberty, or property, without due process of law; nor shall private property be taken for public use, without just compensation.

AMENDMENT 6

CRIMINAL PROCEDURES

IN ALL CRIMINAL prosecutions, the accused shall enjoy the right to a speedy and public trial, by an impartial jury of the State and district wherein the crime shall have been committed, which district shall have been previously ascertained by law, and to be informed of the nature and cause of the accusation; to be confronted with the witnesses against him; to have compulsory process for obtaining witnesses in his favor, and to have the Assistance of Counsel for his defence.

Amendment 7

Civil Procedures

In Suits at common law, where the value in controversy shall exceed twenty dollars, the right of trial by jury shall be preserved, and no fact tried by a jury, shall be otherwise re-examined in any Court of the United States, than according to the rules of the common law.

Amendment 8
Bail and Punishments

Excessive bail shall not be required, nor excessive fines imposed, nor cruel and unusual punishments inflicted.

Amendment 9
People's Rights

THE ENUMERATION in the Constitution, of certain rights, shall not be construed to deny or disparage others retained by the people.

Amendment 10

States' and People's Powers

THE POWERS NOT delegated to the United States by the Constitution, nor prohibited by it to the States, are reserved to the States respectively, or to the people.

Amendment 11
Suits against States

THE JUDICIAL POWER of the United States shall not be construed to extend to any suit in law or equity, commenced or prosecuted against one of the United States by Citizens of another State, or by Citizens or Subjects of any Foreign State.

Amendment 12
Presidential Election

THE ELECTORS SHALL MEET in their respective states and vote by ballot for President and Vice-President, one of whom, at least, shall not be an inhabitant of the same state with themselves; they shall name in their ballots the person voted for as President, and in distinct ballots the person voted for as Vice-President, and they shall make distinct lists of all persons voted for as President, and of all persons voted for as Vice-President, and of the number of votes for each, which lists they shall sign and certify, and transmit sealed to the seat of the government of the United States, directed to the President of the Senate; — the President of the Senate shall, in the presence of the Senate and House of Representatives, open all the certificates and the votes shall then be counted; — The person having the greatest number of votes for President, shall be the President, if such number be a majority of the whole number of Electors appointed; and if no person have such majority, then from the persons having the highest numbers not exceeding three on the list of those voted for as President, the House of Representatives shall choose immediately, by ballot, the President. But in choosing the President, the votes shall be taken by states, the representation from each state having one vote; a quorum for this purpose shall consist of a member or members from two-thirds of the states, and a majority of all the states shall be necessary to a choice. And if the House of Representatives shall not choose a President whenever the right of choice shall devolve upon them, before the fourth day of March next following, then the Vice-President shall act as President, as in case of the death or other constitutional disability of the President. The person having the greatest number of votes as Vice-President, shall be the Vice-President, if such number be a majority of the whole number of Electors appointed, and if no person have a majority, then from the two highest numbers on the list, the Senate shall choose the Vice-President; a quorum for the purpose shall consist of two-thirds of the whole number of Senators, and a majority of the whole number shall be necessary to a choice. But no person constitutionally ineligible to the office of President shall be eligible to that of Vice-President of the United States.

Amendment 13

Slavery Abolition

Section 1

Neither slavery nor involuntary servitude, except as a punishment for crime whereof the party shall have been duly convicted, shall exist within the United States, or any place subject to their jurisdiction.

Section 2

Congress shall have power to enforce this article by appropriate legislation.

AMENDMENT 14

FORMER-SLAVE
PROTECTION

Section 1

All persons born or naturalized in the United States, and subject to the jurisdiction thereof, are citizens of the United States and of the State wherein they reside. No State shall make or enforce any law which shall abridge the privileges or immunities of citizens of the United States; nor shall any State deprive any person of life, liberty, or property, without due process of law; nor deny to any person within its jurisdiction the equal protection of the laws.

Section 2

Representatives shall be apportioned among the several States according to their respective numbers, counting the whole number of persons in each State, excluding Indians not taxed. But when the right to vote at any election for the choice of electors for President and Vice-President of the United States, Representatives in Congress, the Executive and Judicial officers of a State, or the members of the Legislature thereof, is denied to any of the male inhabitants of such State, being twenty-one years of age, and citizens of the United States, or in any way abridged, except for participation in rebellion, or other crime, the basis of representation therein shall be reduced in the proportion which the number of such male citizens shall bear to the whole number of male citizens twenty-one years of age in such State.

Section 3

No person shall be a Senator or Representative in Congress, or elector of President and Vice-President, or hold any office, civil or military, under the United States, or under any State, who, having previously taken an oath, as a member of Congress, or as an officer of the United States, or as a member of any State legislature, or as an executive or judicial officer of any State, to support the Constitution of the United States, shall have engaged in insurrection or rebellion against the same, or given aid or comfort to the enemies thereof. But Congress may by a vote of two-thirds of each House, remove such disability.

Section 4

The validity of the public debt of the United States, authorized by law, including debts incurred for payment of pensions and bounties for services in suppressing insurrection or rebellion, shall not be questioned. But neither the United States nor any State shall assume or pay any debt or obligation incurred in aid of insurrection or rebellion against the United States, or any claim for the loss or emancipation of any slave; but all such debts, obligations and claims shall be held illegal and void.

Section 5

The Congress shall have the power to enforce, by appropriate legislation, the provisions of this article.

Amendment 15

Former-Slave Voting

Section 1

The right of citizens of the United States to vote shall not be denied or abridged by the United States or by any State on account of race, color, or previous condition of servitude —

Section 2

The Congress shall have the power to enforce this article by appropriate legislation.

Amendment 16

National Income Tax

THE CONGRESS SHALL HAVE power to lay and collect taxes on incomes, from whatever source derived, without apportionment among the several States, and without regard to any census or enumeration.

Amendment 17

Senator Election

THE SENATE OF THE United States shall be composed of two Senators from each State, elected by the people thereof, for six years; and each Senator shall have one vote. The electors in each State shall have the qualifications requisite for electors of the most numerous branch of the State legislatures.

When vacancies happen in the representation of any State in the Senate, the executive authority of such State shall issue writs of election to fill such vacancies: Provided, That the legislature of any State may empower the executive thereof to make temporary appointments until the people fill the vacancies by election as the legislature may direct.

This amendment shall not be so construed as to affect the election or term of any Senator chosen before it becomes valid as part of the Constitution.

Amendment 18

PROHIBITION

Section 1

After one year from the ratification of this article the manufacture, sale, or transportation of intoxicating liquors within, the importation thereof into, or the exportation thereof from the United States and all territory subject to the jurisdiction thereof for beverage purposes is hereby prohibited.

Section 2

The Congress and the several States shall have concurrent power to enforce this article by appropriate legislation.

Section 3

This article shall be inoperative unless it shall have been ratified as an amendment to the

Constitution by the legislatures of the several States, as provided in the Constitution, within seven years from the date of the submission hereof to the States by the Congress.

Amendment 19

Women Voting

THE RIGHT OF CITIZENS of the United States to vote shall not be denied or abridged by the United States or by any State on account of sex.

Congress shall have power to enforce this article by appropriate legislation.

AMENDMENT 20

PRESIDENTIAL SUCCESSION

Section 1

The terms of the President and the Vice President shall end at noon on the 20th day of January, and the terms of Senators and Representatives at noon on the 3d day of January, of the years in which such terms would have ended if this article had not been ratified; and the terms of their successors shall then begin.

Section 2

The Congress shall assemble at least once in every year, and such meeting shall begin at noon on the 3d day of January, unless they shall by law appoint a different day.

Section 3

If, at the time fixed for the beginning of the term of the President, the President elect shall have died, the Vice President elect shall become President. If a President shall not have been chosen before the time fixed for the beginning of his term, or if the President elect shall have failed to qualify, then the Vice President elect shall act as President until a President shall have qualified; and the Congress may by law provide for the case wherein neither a President elect nor a Vice President elect shall have qualified, declaring who shall then act as President, or the manner in which one who is to act shall be selected, and such person shall act accordingly until a President or Vice President shall have qualified.

Section 4

The Congress may by law provide for the case of the death of any of the persons from whom the House of Representatives may choose a President whenever the right of choice shall have devolved upon them, and for the case of the death of any of the persons from whom the Senate may choose a Vice President whenever the right of choice shall have devolved upon them.

Section 5

Sections 1 and 2 shall take effect on the 15th day of October following the ratification of this article.

Section 6

This article shall be inoperative unless it shall have been ratified as an amendment to the Constitution by the legislatures of three-fourths of the several States within seven years from the date of its submission.

AMENDMENT 21

PROHIBITION REPEAL

Section 1

The eighteenth article of amendment to the Constitution of the United States is hereby repealed.

Section 2

The transportation or importation into any State, Territory, or possession of the United States for delivery or use therein of intoxicating liquors, in violation of the laws thereof, is hereby prohibited.

Section 3

This article shall be inoperative unless it shall have been ratified as an amendment to the Constitution by conventions in the several States, as provided in the Constitution, within seven years from the date of the submission hereof to the States by the Congress.

Amendment 22

Presidential Term Limit

Section 1

No person shall be elected to the office of the President more than twice, and no person who has held the office of President, or acted as President, for more than two years of a term to which some other person was elected President shall be elected to the office of the President more than once. But this Article shall not apply to any person holding the office of President when this Article was proposed by the Congress, and shall not prevent any person who may be holding the office of President, or acting as President, during the term within which this Article becomes operative from holding the office of President or acting as President during the remainder of such term.

189

Section 2

This article shall be inoperative unless it shall have been ratified as an amendment to the Constitution by the legislatures of three-fourths of the several States within seven years from the date of its submission to the States by the Congress.

Amendment 23

DC Presidential Electors

Section 1

The District constituting the seat of Government of the United States shall appoint in such manner as the Congress may direct:

A number of electors of President and Vice President equal to the whole number of Senators and Representatives in Congress to which the District would be entitled if it were a State, but in no event more than the least populous State; they shall be in addition to those appointed by the States, but they shall be considered, for the purposes of the election of President and Vice President, to be electors appointed by a State; and they shall meet in the District and perform such duties as provided by the twelfth article of amendment.

Section 2

The Congress shall have power to enforce this article by appropriate legislation.

AMENDMENT 24

POLL TAX

Section 1

The right of citizens of the United States to vote in any primary or other election for President or Vice President, for electors for President or Vice President, or for Senator or Representative in Congress, shall not be denied or abridged by the United States or any State by reason of failure to pay any poll tax or other tax.

Section 2

The Congress shall have power to enforce this article by appropriate legislation.

Amendment 25
Presidential Incapacity

Section 1

In case of the removal of the President from office or of his death or resignation, the Vice President shall become President.

Section 2

Whenever there is a vacancy in the office of the Vice President, the President shall nominate a Vice President who shall take office upon confirmation by a majority vote of both Houses of Congress.

Section 3

Whenever the President transmits to the President pro tempore of the Senate and the

Speaker of the House of Representatives his written declaration that he is unable to discharge the powers and duties of his office, and until he transmits to them a written declaration to the contrary, such powers and duties shall be discharged by the Vice President as Acting President.

Section 4

Whenever the Vice President and a majority of either the principal officers of the executive departments or of such other body as Congress may by law provide, transmit to the President pro tempore of the Senate and the Speaker of the House of Representatives their written declaration that the President is unable to discharge the powers and duties of his office, the Vice President shall immediately assume the powers and duties of the office as Acting President.

Thereafter, when the President transmits to the President pro tempore of the Senate and the Speaker of the House of Representatives his written declaration that no inability exists, he shall resume the powers and duties of his office unless the Vice President and a majority of either the principal officers of the executive department or of such other body as Congress may by law provide, transmit within four days to the President pro tempore of the Senate and the Speaker of the House of Representatives their written declaration that the President is unable to discharge the powers and duties of his office. Thereupon Congress shall decide the issue, assembling within forty-eight hours for that purpose if not in session. If the Congress, within twenty-one days after receipt of the latter written declaration, or, if Congress is not in session, within twenty-one days after Congress is required to assemble, determines by two-thirds vote of both Houses that the President is unable to discharge the powers and duties of his office, the Vice President shall continue to discharge the same as Acting President; otherwise, the President shall resume the powers and duties of his office.

AMENDMENT 26

AGE 18 VOTING

Section 1

The right of citizens of the United States, who are eighteen years of age or older, to vote shall not be denied or abridged by the United States or by any State on account of age.

Section 2

The Congress shall have power to enforce this article by appropriate legislation.

AMENDMENT 27
CONGRESSIONAL COMPENSATION

No LAW, VARYING THE compensation for the services of the Senators and Representatives, shall take effect, until an election of Representatives shall have intervened.

PART 3

USA DECLARATION OF INDEPENDENCE[93]

In Congress, July 4, 1776.

The unanimous Declaration of the thirteen united States of America, When in the Course of human events, it becomes necessary for one people to dissolve the political bands which have connected them with another, and to assume among the powers of the earth, the separate and equal station to which the Laws of Nature and of Nature's God entitle them, a decent respect to the opinions of mankind requires that they should declare the causes which impel them to the separation.

We hold these truths to be self-evident, that all men are created equal, that they are endowed by their Creator with certain unalienable Rights, that among these are Life, Liberty and the pursuit of Happiness. — That to secure these rights, Governments are instituted among Men, deriving their just powers from the consent of the governed, — That whenever any Form of Government becomes destructive of these ends, it is the Right of the People to alter or to abolish it, and to institute new Government, laying its foundation on such principles and organizing its powers in such form, as to them shall seem most likely to effect their Safety and Happiness. Prudence, indeed, will dictate that Governments long established should not be changed for light and transient causes; and accordingly all experience hath shewn, that mankind are more disposed to suffer, while evils are sufferable, than to right themselves by abolishing the forms to which they are accustomed. But when a long train of abuses and usurpations, pursuing invariably the same Object evinces a design to reduce them under absolute Despotism, it is their right, it is their duty, to throw off such Government, and to provide new Guards for their future security. — Such has been the patient sufferance of these Colonies; and such is now the necessity which constrains them to alter their former Systems of Government. The history of the present King of

Great Britain is a history of repeated injuries and usurpations, all having in direct object the establishment of an absolute Tyranny over these States. To prove this, let Facts be submitted to a candid world.

He has refused his Assent to Laws, the most wholesome and necessary for the public good.

He has forbidden his Governors to pass Laws of immediate and pressing importance, unless suspended in their operation till his Assent should be obtained; and when so suspended, he has utterly neglected to attend to them.

He has refused to pass other Laws for the accommodation of large districts of people, unless those people would relinquish the right of Representation in the Legislature, a right inestimable to them and formidable to tyrants only.

He has called together legislative bodies at places unusual, uncomfortable, and distant from the depository of their public Records, for the sole purpose of fatiguing them into compliance with his measures.

He has dissolved Representative Houses repeatedly, for opposing with manly firmness his invasions on the rights of the people.

He has refused for a long time, after such dissolutions, to cause others to be elected; whereby the Legislative powers, incapable of Annihilation, have returned to the People at large for their exercise; the State remaining in the mean time exposed to all the dangers of invasion from without, and convulsions within.

He has endeavoured to prevent the population of these States; for that purpose obstructing the Laws for Naturalization of Foreigners; refusing to pass others to encourage their migrations hither, and raising the conditions of new Appropriations of Lands.

He has obstructed the Administration of Justice, by refusing his Assent to Laws for establishing Judiciary powers.

He has made Judges dependent on his Will alone, for the tenure of their offices, and the amount and payment of their salaries.

He has erected a multitude of New Offices, and sent hither swarms of Officers to harrass our people, and eat out their substance.

He has kept among us, in times of peace, Standing Armies without the Consent of our legislatures.

He has affected to render the Military independent of and superior to the Civil power.

He has combined with others to subject us to a jurisdiction foreign to our constitution, and unacknowledged by our laws; giving his Assent to their Acts of pretended Legislation:

For Quartering large bodies of armed troops among us:

For protecting them, by a mock Trial, from punishment for any Murders which they should commit on the Inhabitants of these States:

For cutting off our Trade with all parts of the world:

For imposing Taxes on us without our Consent:

For depriving us in many cases, of the benefits of Trial by Jury:

For transporting us beyond Seas to be tried for pretended offences

For abolishing the free System of English Laws in a neighbouring Province, establishing therein an Arbitrary government, and enlarging its Boundaries so as to render it at once an example and fit instrument for introducing the same absolute rule into these Colonies:

For taking away our Charters, abolishing our most valuable Laws, and altering fundamentally the Forms of our Governments:

For suspending our own Legislatures, and declaring themselves invested with power to legislate for us in all cases whatsoever.

He has abdicated Government here, by declaring us out of his Protection and waging War against us.

He has plundered our seas, ravaged our Coasts, burnt our towns, and destroyed the lives of our people.

He is at this time transporting large Armies of foreign Mercenaries to compleat the works of death, desolation and tyranny, already begun with circumstances of Cruelty & perfidy scarcely paralleled in the most barbarous ages, and totally unworthy the Head of a civilized nation.

He has constrained our fellow Citizens taken Captive on the high Seas to bear Arms against their Country, to become the executioners of their friends and Brethren, or to fall themselves by their Hands.

He has excited domestic insurrections amongst us, and has endeavoured to bring on the inhabitants of our frontiers, the merciless Indian Savages, whose known rule of warfare, is an undistinguished destruction of all ages, sexes and conditions.

In every stage of these Oppressions We have Petitioned for Redress in the most humble terms: Our repeated Petitions have been answered only by repeated injury. A Prince whose character is thus marked by every act which may define a Tyrant, is unfit to be the ruler of a free people.

Nor have We been wanting in attentions to our Brittish brethren. We have warned them from time to time of attempts by their legislature to extend an unwarrantable jurisdiction over us. We have reminded them of the circumstances of our emigration and settlement here. We have appealed to their native justice and magnanimity, and we have conjured them by the ties of our common kindred to disavow these usurpations, which, would inevitably interrupt our connections and correspondence. They too have been deaf to the voice of justice and of consanguinity. We must, therefore, acquiesce in the necessity, which denounces our Separation, and hold them, as we hold the rest of mankind, Enemies in War, in Peace Friends.

We, therefore, the Representatives of the united States of America, in General Congress, Assembled, appealing to the Supreme Judge of the world for the rectitude of our intentions, do, in the Name, and by Authority of the good People of these Colonies, solemnly publish and declare, That these United Colonies are, and of Right ought to be Free and Independent States; that they are Absolved from all Allegiance to the

British Crown, and that all political connection between them and the State of Great Britain, is and ought to be totally dissolved; and that as Free and Independent States, they have full Power to levy War, conclude Peace, contract Alliances, establish Commerce, and to do all other Acts and Things which Independent States may of right do. And for the support of this Declaration, with a firm reliance on the protection of divine Providence, we mutually pledge to each other our Lives, our Fortunes and our sacred Honor.

REFERENCES

1   Rabushka, Alvin. *Taxation in Colonial America.*
Princeton University Press, 2010, Scribd p. 1437.

2   Lindert, Peter H., and Jeffrey G. Williamson. *Unequal Gains: American Growth and Inequality since 1700.*
Princeton University Press, 2016, Scribd pp. 107–108.

3   Wood, Gordon S. *The Radicalism of the American Revolution.* Alfred A. Knopf, 1991, p. 169.

4   Barnett, Randy E. *Our Republican Constitution: Securing the Liberty and Sovereignty of We the People.*
Broadside Books, 2016, pp. 182–184.

5   Barnett, Randy E. *Our Republican Constitution: Securing the Liberty and Sovereignty of We the People.*
Broadside Books, 2016, pp. 167–168.

6   Wallis, John Joseph. "American Government Finance in the Long Run: 1790 to 1990." *Journal of Economic Perspectives*, vol. 14, no. 1, 2000, pp. 61–82.

7   Simon, Julian L. "More People, Greater Wealth, More Resources, Healthier Environment." *Economic Affairs*, vol. 14, no. 3, Apr. 1994, pp. 22–29.

[8] Higgs, Robert. *Neither Liberty nor Safety: Fear, Ideology, and the Growth of Government.* The Independent Institute, 2007, Scribd p. 58.

[9] Hamburger, Philip. *The Administrative Threat.* Encounter Books, 2017.

[10] Higgs, Robert. *Crisis and Leviathan: Critical Episodes in the Growth of American Government.* Oxford University Press, 1987.

[11] "List of United States Presidential Elections by Electoral College Margin." *Wikipedia,* 13 June 2017, en.wikipedia.org/wiki/List_of_United_States_presidential_elections_by_Electoral_College_margin. Accessed 28 June 2017.

[12] Gienapp, William E. *The Origins of the Republican Party, 1852–1856.* Oxford University Press, 1987, p. 4, pp. 443–448.

[13] The Episcopal Church. *The Book of Common Prayer.* Church Publishing Incorporated, 2007, pp. 41–42, www.episcopalchurch.org/files/book_of_common_prayer.pdf. Accessed 22 Nov. 2017.

[14] "Conservative Review – Scorecard." *Conservative Review.com,* www.conservativereview.com/scorecard. Accessed 29 Jan. 2017.

[15] Skowronek, Stephen, et al, editors. *The Progressives' Century: Political Reform, Constitutional Government, and the Modern American State.* Yale University Press, 2016.

[16] Barnett, Randy E. *Our Republican Constitution: Securing the Liberty and Sovereignty of We the People.* Broadside Books, 2016, pp. 19–22.

[17] *The Bible.* New International Version, 2011, Judges 17:6, Judges 21:25.

[18] "Multiyear Download of US Government Spending 1792–2021." *usgovermentdebt.com,* www.usgovernment debt.us/download_multi_year_1792_2021USp_ 18s2li001mcn_H0t. Accessed 12 Feb. 2017.

[19] Eisenach, Eldon. "A Progressive Conundrum. Federal Constitution, National State, and Popular Sovereignty." *The Progressives' Century: Political Reform, Constitutional Government, and the Modern American State,* edited by Stephen Skowronek et al, Yale University Press, 2016, pp. 16–37; p. 16.

[20] Ilzetzki, Ethan, et al. "How Big (Small?) Are Fiscal Multipliers?" *Journal of Monetary Economics,* vol. 60, no. 2, 2013, pp. 239–254.

[21] Reinhart, Carmen M., and Kenneth S. Rogoff. *This Time Is Different: Eight Centuries of Financial Folly.* Princeton University Press, 2009.

[22] Eastwood, Clint, actor. *The Outlaw Josey Wales.* Directed by Clint Eastwood, Warner Brothers, 1976.

[23] Reynolds, Alan. "Big Government, Big Recession." *The Wall Street Journal,* Eastern ed., vol. 254, no. 44, 21 Aug. 2009, p. A13.

[24] "Government." *Gallup,* www.gallup.com/poll/27286/ government.aspx. Accessed 12 Feb. 2017.

[25] "US Conservatives Outnumber Liberals by Narrowing Margin." *Gallup,* 3 Jan. 2017, www.gallup .com/poll/201152/conservative-liberal-gap-continues-narrow-tuesday.aspx. Accessed 13 Feb. 2017.

[26] Hickey, Jennifer G. "Republicans Build on Their Dominance in State Legislatures." *FoxNews.com*, 18 Nov. 2016, www.foxnews.com/politics/2016/11/18/republicans-build-on-their-dominance-in-state-legislatures.html. Accessed 13 Feb. 2017.

[27] Kohn, Richard H. "The Constitution and National Security: The Intent of the Framers." *The United States Military under the Constitution of the United States, 1789–1989,* edited by Richard H. Kohn, New York University Press, 1991, pp. 61–94.

[28] Barnett, Randy E. *Our Republican Constitution: Securing the Liberty and Sovereignty of We the People.* Broadside Books, 2016, p. 19, pp. 22–26.

[29] Barnett, Randy E. *Our Republican Constitution: Securing the Liberty and Sovereignty of We the People.* Broadside Books, 2016, p. 44.

[30] Epstein, Richard Allen. *Simple Rules for a Complex World.* Harvard University Press, 1995.

[31] Hamburger, Philip. *Is Administrative Law Unlawful?* University of Chicago Press, 2014.

[32] Darrow, Jonathan J. "Pharmaceutical Efficacy: The Illusory Legal Standard." *Washington and Lee Law Review,* vol. 70, no. 4, 2013, pp. 2073–2136, scholarlycommons.law.wlu.edu/cgi/viewcontent.cgi?article=4358&context=wlulr. Accessed 22 Nov. 2017.

[33] Higgs, Robert. "Banning a Risky Product Cannot Improve Any Consumer's Welfare (Properly Understood), with Applications to FDA Testing Requirements." *The Review of Austrian Economics,* vol. 7, no. 2, 1994, pp. 3–20.

[34] Klein, Daniel B., and Alexander Taborrok. "Theory, Evidence and Examples of FDA Harm." *FDAReview.org,* The Independent Institute, 2016, www.fdareview.org/ 05_harm.php. Accessed 25 Sep. 2017.

[35] Somin, Ilya. *Democracy and Political Ignorance: Why Smaller Government Is Smarter.* 2nd ed., Stanford University Press, 2013, pp. 119–154.

[36] *U.S. Constitution.* Amend. V, and Amend. XIV, Sec. 1.

[37] *U.S. Constitution.* Art. VI, Cl. 3.

[38] Koch, Charles G. *Good Profit: How Creating Value for Others Built One of the World's Most Successful Companies.* Crown Business, 2015.

[39] Hülsmann, Jörg Guido. "Has Fractional-Reserve Banking Really Passed the Market Test?" *The Independent Review,* vol. 7, no. 3, 2003, pp. 399–422, www.independent.org/pdf/tir/tir_07_3_hulsmann.pdf. Accessed 22 Nov. 2017.

[40] Higgs, Robert. "What Got Us into and out of the Great Depression?" *Neither Liberty nor Safety: Fear, Ideology, and the Growth of Government,* The Independent Institute, 2007, Scribd pp. 176–212.

[41] Horwitz, Steven. "Causes and Cures of the Great Recession." *Economic Affairs,* vol. 32, no. 3, 2012, pp. 65–69.

[42] Cochrane, John H. "Toward a Run-Free Financial System." *Across the Great Divide: New Perspectives on the Financial Crisis,* edited by Martin Neil Baily and John B. Taylor, Hoover Institution Press, 2014, pp. 197–250.

[43] McGee, Robert W. "The Case for Privatizing Money." *The Asian Economic Review,* vol. 30, no. 2, Aug. 1988, pp. 258–273.

[44] Hülsmann, Jörg Guido. *Ethics of Money Production.* Ludwig von Mises Institute, 2008, pp. 60–62, www.mises .net/sites/default/files/The%20Ethics%20of%20 Money%20Production_2.pdf. Accessed 22 Nov. 2017.

[45] McCandless, George T., Jr., and Warren E. Weber. "Some Monetary Facts." *Federal Reserve Bank of Minneapolis Quarterly Review,* vol. 19, no. 3, 1995, pp. 2–11, www.minneapolisfed.org/research/qr/qr1931.pdf. Accessed 22 Nov. 2017.

[46] Harrison, Mark. "The Economics of World War II: An Overview." *The Economics of World War II: Six Great Powers in International Comparison,* edited by Mark Harrison, Cambridge University Press, 2000, pp. 1–42.

[47] Bork, Robert H. "The Impossibility of Finding Welfare Rights in the Constitution." *Washington University Law Quarterly,* vol. 1979, no. 3, 1979, pp. 695–701, openscholarship.wustl.edu/cgi/viewcontent.cgi?article= 2535&context=law_lawreview. Accessed 22 Nov. 2017.

[48] Hoke, Candice. "State Discretion under New Federal Welfare Legislation: Illusion, Reality and a Federalism-Based Constitutional Challenge." *Stanford Law & Policy Review,* vol. 9, no. 1, 1998, pp. 115–130.

[49] Coenen, Dan T. "The Filibuster and the Framing: Why the Cloture Rule Is Unconstitutional and What to Do About It." *Boston College Law Review,* vol. 55, no. 1, 2014, pp. 39–92, bclawreview.org/files/2014/01/02_ coenen.pdf. Accessed 22 Nov. 2017.

[50] Havrylyshyn, Oleh, et al. "25 Years of Reforms in Ex-Communist Countries: Fast and Extensive Reforms Led to Higher Growth and More Political Freedom." *Policy Analysis*, no. 795, 2016, object.cato .org/sites/cato.org/files/pubs/pdf/pa795_2.pdf. Accessed 22 Nov. 2017.

[51] "Forecasts, Macro Data, Transition Indicators." *European Bank for Reconstruction and Development*, www.ebrd.com/what-we-do/economic-research-and-data/data/forecasts-macro-data-transition-indicators .html. Accessed 18 Oct. 2017.

[52] Story, Joseph. *Commentaries on the Constitution of the United States: With a Preliminary Review of the Constitutional History of the Colonies and States Before the Adoption of the Constitution.* 4th ed., with notes and additions, vol. I, Boston, Little, Brown, and Company, 1873, p. 265, ia600304.us.archive.org/17/items/commentaries onco01storuoft/commentariesonco01storuoft.pdf. Accessed 22 Nov. 2017.

[53] Mathews, Mitford M., editor. *A Dictionary of Americanisms on Historical Principles.* Vol. I, University of Chicago Press, 1951, pp. 198–199.

[54] *U.S. Constitution.* Amend. X.

[55] Eno, Robert. "Trump Supporters Should Be Thanking Senator Mike Lee and Ken Cuccinelli." *ConservativeReview.com*, 18 July 2016, www.conservative review.com/commentary/2016/07/trump-supporters-should-be-thanking-senator-mike-lee-and-ken-cuccinelli#sthash.jka6iYn2.dpuf. Accessed 14 Feb. 2017.

[56] "Republican Party Presidential Debates and Forums, 2016." *Wikipedia.org*, 6 May 2017, en.wikipedia.org/wiki/Republican_Party_presidential_debates_and_forums,_2016. Accessed 7 May 2017.

[57] Van Zandt, Dave, editor. *Media Bias / Fact Check.* MBFC News, 2015, mediabiasfactcheck.com/. Accessed 7 May 2017.

[58] Gates, Bill. "Content Is King." *Microsoft.com*, 3 Jan. 1996, web.archive.org/web/20010126005200/http://www.microsoft.com/billgates/columns/1996essay/essay960103.asp. Accessed 18 Feb. 2017.

[59] "114th Congress Guide and Elections Data by District." 24 Oct. 2016, docs.google.com/spreadsheets/d/1lGZQi9AxPHjE0RllvhNEBHFvrJGlnmC43AXnR8dwHMc/edit#gid=1978064869. Accessed 6 May 2017.

[60] "District of Columbia's At-Large Congressional District." *Wikipedia.org*, 15 Feb. 2017, en.wikipedia.org/wiki/District_of_Columbia%27s_at-large_congressional_district. Accessed 9 May 2017.

[61] Elliott, Scott. "2016 Republican Nomination Delegates." *ElectionProjection.com*, 8 June 2016, www.electionprojection.com/republican-nomination-delegates/. Accessed 6 May 2017.

[62] Leip, David. "2016 Presidential Republican Primary Election Data—National." *Dave Leip's Atlas of U.S. Presidential Elections*, 2016, uselectionatlas.org/RESULTS/data.php?year=2016&datatype=national&def=1&f=0&off=0&elect=2/. Accessed 9 May 2017.

[63] Ericsson, Anders, and Robert Pool. *Peak: Secrets from the New Science of Expertise.* Houghton Mifflin Harcourt, 2016, pp. 250–253.

[64] Deslauriers, Louis, et al. "Improved Learning in a Large-Enrollment Physics Class." *Science,* vol. 332, no. 6031, 2011, pp. 862–864.

[65] Bolton, Robert. *People Skills.* Touchstone, 2009, pp. 262–314.

[66] Luo, Shanhong, and Eva C. Klohnen. "Assortative Mating and Marital Quality in Newlyweds: A Couple-Centered Approach." *Journal of Personality and Social Psychology,* vol. 88, no. 2, 2005, pp. 304–326.

[67] Anderson, Cameron, et al. "Emotional Convergence between People over Time." *Journal of Personality and Social Psychology,* vol. 84, no. 5, 2003, pp. 1054–1068.

[68] Kuhn, Thomas S. *The Structure of Scientific Revolutions.* 2nd ed., enlarged, The University of Chicago Press, 1970, pp. 150–159.

[69] Porter, Michael. "The Economic Performance of Regions." *Regional Studies,* vol. 37, nos. 6–7, 2003, pp. 549–578.

[70] Field, Alexander J. "Economic Growth and Recovery in the United States: 1919–1941." *The Great Depression of the 1930s: Lessons for Today,* edited by Nicholas Crafts and Peter Fearon, Oxford University Press, 2013, pp. 358–394.

[71] Field, Alexander J. *A Great Leap Forward: 1930s Depression and US Economic Growth.* Yale University Press, 2011.

[72] Powell, Jim. *FDR's Folly: How Roosevelt and His New Deal Prolonged the Great Depression.* Crown, 2007.

[73] Hargadon, Andrew B. "Firms as Knowledge Brokers: Lessons in Pursuing Continuous Innovation." *California Management Review,* vol. 40, no. 3, 1998, pp. 209–227.

[74] Anderson, Michael L. *After Phrenology*. MIT Press, 2014, pp. 232–238.

[75] Seth, Anil K., and Karl J. Friston. "Active Interoceptive Inference and the Emotional Brain." *Philosophical Transactions of the Royal Society B: Biological Sciences,* vol. 371, no. 1708, 2016, 20160007, rstb.royalsociety publishing.org/content/royptb/371/1708/20160007 .full.pdf. Accessed 22 Nov. 2017.

[76] Blackburn, Joseph D., et al. "Improving Speed and Productivity of Software Development: A Global Survey of Software Developers." *IEEE Transactions on Software Engineering,* vol. 22, no. 12, 1996, pp. 875–885.

[77] Curry, Robert. *Common Sense Nation: Unlocking the Forgotten Power of the American Idea*. Encounter Books, 2015.

[78] Rothbard, Murray N. "Origins of the Welfare State in America." *Journal of Libertarian Studies,* vol. 12, no. 2, 1996, pp. 193-232, mises-media.s3.amazonaws .com/12_2_1_0.pdf?file=1&type=document. Accessed 19 July 2018.

[79] Lindert, Peter H., and Jeffrey G. Williamson. *Unequal Gains: American Growth and Inequality since 1700*. Princeton University Press, 2016, Scribd pp. 61, 158.

[80] Simon, Julian L. "More People, Greater Wealth, More Resources, Healthier Environment." *Economic Affairs,* vol. 14, no. 3, Apr. 1994, pp. 22–29.

[81] Ritchie, Hannah. "What the History of London's Air Pollution Can Tell Us about the Future of Today's Growing Megacities." *Our World in Data,* 20 June 2017,

ourworldindata.org/london-air-pollution/. Accessed 15 Aug. 2017.

[82] Carson, Richard T., et al. "The Relationship between Air Pollution Emissions and Income: US Data." *Environment and Development Economics,* vol. 2, no. 4, 1997, pp. 433–450.

[83] *Field of Dreams.* Directed by Phil Alden Robinson, Gordon Company, 1989.

[84] *Official 2016 Presidential General Election Results.* Federal Election Commission, 20 Jan. 2017, transition. fec.gov/pubrec/fe2016/2016presgeresults.pdf. Accessed 19 July 2018.

[85] Hardy, Quentin. "Google Thinks Small." *Forbes,* vol. 176, no. 10, 14 Nov. 2005, pp. 198–202, www.forbes .com/forbes/2005/1114/198.html#5ce26ef33416. Accessed 19 July 2018.

[86] *Locke and Smith Foundation.* The YOUNG Conservatives of America, 2018, lockeandsmith.org. Accessed 19 July 2018.

[87] Franklin, Benjamin. "JOIN, or DIE." *The Philadelphia Gazette,* 9 May 1754, www.loc.gov/pictures/item/ 2002695523/. Accessed 18 July 2018.

[88] *U.S. Declaration of Independence.*

[89] "The Constitution of the United States: A Transcription." *Archives.gov,* 10 Jan. 2017, www.archives .gov/founding-docs/constitution-transcript. Accessed 8 Feb. 2017.

[90] "The Bill of Rights: A Transcription." *Archives.gov,* 6 Oct. 2016, www.archives.gov/founding-docs/bill-of-rights-transcript. Accessed 8 Feb. 2017.

[91] "The Constitution: Amendments 11–27." *Archives .gov,* 6 Oct. 2016, www.archives.gov/founding-docs/ amendments-11-27. Accessed 8 Feb. 2017.

[92] Brady, Robert A., editor. *The Constitution of the United States of America As Amended.* House Doc. 110–50, Government Printing Office, 2007, www.gpo.gov/ fdsys/pkg/CDOC-110hdoc50/pdf/CDOC-110hdoc50 .pdf. Accessed 5 May 2017.

[93] "Declaration of Independence: A Transcription." *Archives.gov,* 19 Jan. 2017, www.archives.gov/founding- docs/declaration-transcript. Accessed 8 Feb. 2017.

INDEX

CPSIA information can be obtained
at www.ICGtesting.com
Printed in the USA
LVHW090233260119
605321LV00003B/64/P